FOUNDED
BY
FAITH

THE FOUND BOYS

Inspiring and Igniting Your Rise
From Teen Boy to Mighty Man.

Founded by Faith.

Welded by Wisdom.

Built by God.

by

YAPHETT K. POWELL, J.D., M.B.A.

Published by hope*books
2217 Matthews Township Pkwy
Suite D302
Matthews, NC 28105
www.hopebooks.com

hope*books is a division of hope*media

Printed in the United States of America

First paperback edition.
Paperback ISBN: 979-8-89185-301-0
Hardcover ISBN: 979-8-89185-146-7
Ebook ISBN: 979-8-89185-147-4
Library of Congress Number: 2024951047

hope∗books
hopebooks.com
Because the world needs your hope-filled
words now more than ever.

ENDORSEMENTS

~~~

"I've built my career on helping driven men overcome adversity, unlock their best, and win more often. That's why I'm excited about Yaphett K. Powell's book, *Founded by Faith: The Found Boys*. As a father to a teenage boy, I honor Yaphett for writing in a way that inspires young men to show up with confidence, tackle their fears, and stay grounded in their faith. Yaphett's blend of storytelling and actionable lessons empowers teenage boys to face life with strength and resilience. It's an incredible resource that I wholeheartedly endorse for any young man aiming to live a life of purpose and impact."

–JAMES REID, International Human Performance Strategist, Host, Coming Up Clutch with J.R.™, Founder, The Clutch Club™

"As a licensed psychotherapist, author, and mother of two young adult men, I understand how crucial it is for teenage boys to have resources that support their emotional and spiritual growth. Yaphett K. Powell's *Founded by Faith: The Found Boys* is a book I would have given my sons in their adolescence. Yaphett's authentic, impactful, and relatable voice is a lighthouse for young men, illuminating the path to building a life of faith on a firm foundation. Yaphett's captivating words remind young men, especially those feeling a little lost, that they have a purpose, a future, and a guide as they navigate the often difficult path from adolescence to adulthood. Through his own story of resilience and strength, forged from a difficult start, he shows teen boys that despite not having all the resources or even a father to show them the way, they have a Heavenly Father. Yaphett outlines a foundation available to them to become thriving, grounded, fearless men equipped with the tools to overcome life's challenges. This is an essential read for any teenage boy."

–DR. ZOE SHAW, licensed psychotherapist, motivational speaker, host of the Stronger in the Difficult Places podcast, author of A Year of Self-Care, and founder of www.DrZoeShaw.com

"In my years coaching at universities and working with the Fellowship of Christian Athletes, I've always valued resources that equip young men to navigate life with faith and resilience. Yaphett K. Powell's *Founded by Faith: The Found Boys* does just that. It's a guide that empowers teenage boys to face their unique challenges while remaining true to themselves and their faith. Yaphett's thoughtful approach and practical insights make this book a must-have for parents, coaches, and mentors who want to see their boys grow into confident, courageous, and faith-led young men."

—**MARK WRACHER**, former Director of the Fellowship of Christian Athletes (FCA) in Ohio, Los Angeles, Atlanta, and Tennessee, former assistant football coach at Texas Southern University and Tennessee State University, and former quarterback at Vanderbilt University

ACKNOWLEDGEMENTS

"I can do all things through Christ who strengthens me."
–Philippians 4:13, NKJV

I acknowledge Jesus Christ for strengthening and empowering me to write this book. I also acknowledge my awesome mom, Shirley, and my best friend, Bashere, for inspiring me to become an author. You both are my author inspirations!

This book is dedicated to God, my two kind and good teenagers (who both inspire me to be the best dad I can be), my beloved younger brother, my large and loving extended family, and my close friends.

This book is also dedicated to my readers around the world... **YOU**. As I have pursued God's plans for my life, I have encountered many obstacles and setbacks, but as I wrote this book for all of you, I realized that it was all for God's good and glory. He brought me to this position as an author so I could help you and many other young people just like you (Genesis 50:20).

CONTENTS

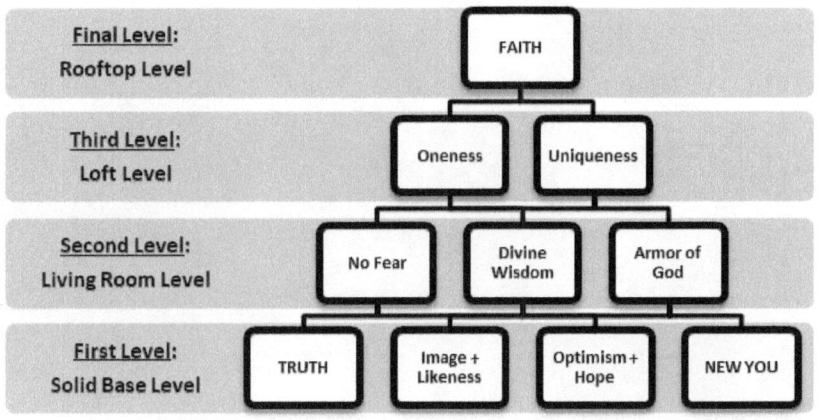

Final Level: Rooftop Level	FAITH			
Third Level: Loft Level	Oneness	Uniqueness		
Second Level: Living Room Level	No Fear	Divine Wisdom	Armor of God	
First Level: Solid Base Level	TRUTH	Image + Likeness	Optimism + Hope	NEW YOU

PROLOGUE

YOU MATTER

To all you teen boys out there feeling lost, trying to find your way through life, figuring out who you are and the kind of man you want to be...

Maybe you feel like no one understands you or cares about you, or maybe you simply feel unmotivated or uninspired...

There is HOPE.

What if... someone showed you the way?
What if... someone showed you the kind of man you were created and intended to be?
What if... someone told you the truth about who you are?

The truth is... YOU matter. You are unique and special. You are here for a purpose. The truth is that you are a son of the Most High God.

Until now, you might've felt lost, but now you are found. You just picked up a book that aims to help you find your way in life. You can become part of a cool community and transformational team: a worldwide community of good guys who want to improve their life and help others do the same. Welcome to The Found Boys. We aim to inspire and ignite teen boys to become mighty young men. Founded by Faith. Welded by Wisdom. Built by God.

YOUR STORY MATTERS

You may be young and in your teens, but does any of this sound familiar to you?

You are growing up without your dad. Maybe he left or was never there, or maybe he is around but mostly absent, or maybe you have a stepdad.

Your mom is your closest family member (or your grandparents or your siblings).

You are growing up in a poor or rough neighborhood.

You just moved to a new neighborhood, and you are having trouble making friends.

You face daily battles with bullies or kids behaving badly at school or online, even when you're minding your own business and staying out of trouble.

You are in high school, and you are already working part-time jobs in addition to going to school.

You don't know what you want to do for a career after you graduate high school.

You don't know if you want to go to college or you are having trouble getting into the college that you want to go to.

You feel like no one understands you or cares about you.

You feel unmotivated or uninspired.

You feel lost.

If any of that sounds familiar to you, then you and I have a lot in common. I experienced or felt all of those things at some point in my teenage years.

When I think back to my teens, I remember that my mom (Shirley), granddaddy and grandma (Eugene and Lula Mae), and my large and loving extended Powell Family always taught me three valuable lessons that helped me get through life and succeed:

FAITH. EDUCATION. WORK. (I like to say they taught me a "F.E.W." things!)

Faith: You can live a better life through faith in God through Jesus Christ.

Education: You can live a better life with a good education, whether it's a formal education in schools, an informal education from continuously learning new things on your own, or both.

Work: You can live a better life by working hard and working smart at everything you do, whether it's a business venture, a paid job, or daily chores.

Through those life lessons and that family framework for success, I discovered and developed my own unique God-given purpose and power over the years as I grew into a man through the following principles:

PRAYER. PROACTIVITY. PERSEVERANCE.

Today, I approach life with a new purpose that is powered by inspiring positivity, optimism, and hope as a new man through faith in God. But it wasn't always that way, especially in my teens, growing up without my biological father and dealing with a difficult stepdad. As I journeyed from a lost teen to a new man, my life took many stormy twists and turns. However, through faith:

- I turned my failures into victories, including going back to college to successfully earn three separate university degrees with various honors and awards — after initially flunking out when I was 19 years old.

  Specifically, I endured, never gave up, and earned degrees from three of the best universities in the world over the course of more than a decade: a B.S. from the University of Florida in 1998, a J.D. from the University of Miami School of Law in 2001, and an M.B.A. from the University of California, Los Angeles (UCLA) Anderson School of Management in 2011. To bring my academic comeback full circle, I also became a university professor at one of the most prestigious law schools in the country: the University of Southern California (USC) Gould School of Law. Not many people can say they're a Gator, Hurricane, Bruin, and Trojan wrapped in one!

- I learned to selflessly serve and lead others, to tirelessly fight for what's right, and to be a positive light to others in dark times.

  For example, I survived and thrived through some of the darkest times in my life by protecting my family through three different major financial disasters between 2009-2024. Each time, I was blindsided and unexpectedly lost large amounts of financial assets and income due to factors outside of my control, so I had to hustle to get back on my feet to provide for my family. As a dad with two kids, I chose to have faith that God would help me overcome instead of being depressed and defeated. And so, during each financial crisis, I served my family tirelessly, supported them emotionally and financially, and cared for their needs above my own.

- I rose up to become an excellent Christian lawyer and leader who is strong and courageous in the face of adversity and trouble.

Despite my academic and financial setbacks, I reached the heights of Corporate America by working my way up the Corporate Ladder to become a successful Vice President, corporate executive, and attorney at some of the biggest and best companies and law firms in the world. I succeeded despite people and society doubting and challenging me because of their own preconceived notions and prejudices about what an African-American man is capable of achieving.

In the world's view, my positive and prayerful proactivity and perseverance have brought me from being an "at-risk youth growing up without a dad" in a poor, disadvantaged "hood" in Florida to a successful L.A. lawyer and business executive. I now live and work in one of the wealthiest neighborhoods in California, where Apple, Google, Amazon, Meta, TikTok, and other leading technology and media companies have offices (ever heard of them?!).

More importantly, in God's View, it has brought me to share His message with you... **THE FOUND BOYS**.

But, enough about me. So, what's your story?

YOU ARE CHOSEN

To this point, you might not have thought a lot about your own story, but we all have a hero origin story. You know... those stories about how your favorite superhero originally got his powers and decided to use them for good. Both Peter Parker and Miles Morales became Spider-Man after they got bit by a radioactive spider, and Peter lost his father figure, Uncle Ben, in a tragic crime that he could've stopped. Kal-El became Super-man after his biological parents on Krypton sent him to Earth to save his life, and his earthly parents took him in and adopted him as their son, mild-mannered Clark Kent, while the power of the Earth's sun gave him superior superpowers. And the list goes on.

When I was a teen, I was a big superhero fan (actually, who am I kidding? I still am!). I remember seeing a guy wearing this really cool superhero t-shirt that ultimately strengthened my faith in God and Jesus Christ. This cool shirt had a picture of all the earth's best superheroes (Spider-Man, Superman, Batman, Captain America, etc.) crowded together in a room with Jesus at the front of the room, and the others were all listening closely to what Jesus had to say.

The shirt had a simple but powerful message that summa-rized the story that Jesus was sharing with the crowd of super-heroes in the room. Written in a short comic book word bubble, Jesus said, "...And that's how I saved the world."

In fact, Jesus has always been pretty clear that He "came to seek and save those who are lost" (Luke 19:10).

So, you should know this simple truth about your own story:

God chose you. Specifically, Jesus said: "I chose you. I appointed you to go and produce lasting fruit, so that the Father will give you whatever you ask for, using my name" (John 15:16).

God gave you "superpowers" that are your own unique gifts and talents, and as an important step in your growth, He wants you to do good: Win God's way. Win with wisdom and triumph with truth. Defeat the lies of the enemy spiritual forces that roam this world and attack innocent people.

As part of God's "superteam," we should all actively use our God-given gifts for good. In a world desperate for hope, we all have the honor of doing our part for God's glory and being part of His story.

When you use your unique God-given gifts and talents for your God-given purpose, God often calls you to be a hero in your own unique way. You don't need to do BIG things—even the smallest acts, such as helping out your parents or friends, are heroic in God's eyes. This is what Jesus meant when He said, "Go and produce lasting fruit."

Save the world. Save lives. Step out into faith and do what God has called you to do. *You* get to be a part of God's great story.

Don't believe me? Just read about Joseph, Moses, and other young people in the Bible who didn't grow up with their birth parents because of danger in the world at the time, but who grew up to become great heroes and save many lives for God's glory.

If you don't know Joseph, know that he was betrayed in his teenage years by his jealous brothers. They threw him into a pit and initially left him to die, but later sold him as a slave to foreigners while lying to their father about what happened to him. As he grew up in the foreign land of Egypt, he was falsely accused by his boss's wife when he refused to do dishonorable things with her, and he was thrown into jail unjustly.

Despite these extraordinary trials and troubles, Joseph still rose to become one of the wisest and most successful men and leaders in Egypt, second-in-charge only to the king of Egypt, Pharaoh. As Pharaoh's second-in-charge, Joseph saved the whole known world from a severe multi-year famine. And during this widespread famine, he found and reconciled with his brothers and father after decades apart. In one of the greatest acts of forgiveness ever, after all that Joseph had been through because of his brothers, Joseph said to them when he found them, "You intended to harm me, but God intended it all for good. He brought me to this position so I could save the lives of many people" (Genesis 50:20).

And if you don't know Moses, he grew up without his father, as his birth mother gave him up as a baby to protect his life. This decision was made due to death threats against his family because of their Israelite ethnicity. Ultimately, he was raised as a foster child by the royal Egyptian family. After he unwittingly killed an Egyptian man while trying to save two Israelites, he lost everything he had, was cast out of society, and lived in exile for many years.

Despite all of that terrible turmoil, God still called Moses back from exile later in life to lead the Israelites out of slavery and to their promised land, write the Ten Commandments, and become one of the leading founding fathers of humanity's faith in God.

God uses Found Boys. Are you ready to start your hero journey and learn more about your unique story for God's glory?

***

THE FOUND BOYS - BUILDING PROJECT:

THE HOUSE OF FAITH

~~~

"Everyone then who hears these words of mine and does them will *be like a wise man who built his house on the rock*. And the rain fell, and the floods came, and the winds blew and beat on that house, but it did not fall, because it had been *founded on the rock*."

–Matthew 7:24-26, ESV (emphasis added)

***

N ow that you've chosen to embark on your new journey, the first step is to understand your unique building project: the "House of Faith." You're probably asking yourself... what is the House of Faith?

IT'S YOU

As you learn and apply the life lessons in this book, you will be building the best and greatest version of yourself. In other words, you will be building your very own House of Faith.

Here's what I mean: when I was a teen, sometimes I felt lost because I grew up poor in a rough neighborhood without my dad. I went through many difficult times without a father to guide me on how to be a man and how to navigate the challenges and storms in my life. But thanks to God, I was blessed to have an awesome mom, grandparents, and large extended family (cousins, aunts, and uncles) who loved God, loved each other, loved their neighbors, and had faith. All of these amazing and wonderful people in my life taught me what it means to have faith and how it could help me live my best life ever.

As I grew up, I leaned into my faith by trusting God, accepting Jesus, praying by myself and with others, finding a solid Christian church and community, and reading the Bible and other good books and devotionals by Christian authors. From all of this, I learned valuable life lessons. These valuable lessons helped me to improve my life and empowered me to rise to become a successful lawyer and business executive and, most importantly, a dad to two teens of my own. Trust me, I didn't always clearly see how I would succeed at fulfilling my dreams and growing into the man that God created me to be. You might feel the same way right now, and there might not be anyone in your life who shows you what you are capable of... I hope this book can do that for you.

So, to help you, I've summed up these valuable lessons into a four-level, foundational framework I call "The House of Faith."

The House of Faith is a supremely strong structure... A house that is so strong that when the heavy storms come, it stands tall and does not fall. It is a framework for you to build the foundation for the greatest version of your unique life.

In this book, you will learn ten valuable life lessons that will serve as building blocks for this supremely strong structure and foundation for your life. In fact, the ten building blocks spell out the word F.O.U.N.D.A.T.I.O.N.:

FAITH
Oneness
Uniqueness
No Fear: Be Strong & Courageous
Divine Wisdom
Armor of God
TRUTH (The Cornerstone)
Image + Likeness
Optimism + Hope
NEW YOU

For inspiration to build your own House of Faith, just know that Jesus specifically said:

"I will show you what it's like when someone comes to me, listens to my teaching, and then follows it. It is like a person building a house who digs deep and *lays the foundation on solid rock*. When the floodwaters rise and break against that house, *it stands firm because it is well built*.

But anyone who hears and doesn't obey is like a person who builds a house right on the ground, *without a foundation*. When the floods sweep down against that house, *it will collapse into a heap of ruins*."

–Luke 6:47-49 (emphasis added)

So, let's begin to lay your F.O.U.N.D.A.T.I.O.N. on solid rock. Here is the blueprint:

THE BLUEPRINT

FAITH

Oneness | Uniqueness

No Fear | Divine Wisdom | Armor of God

TRUTH (The Cornerstone) | Image + Likeness | Optimism + Hope | NEW YOU

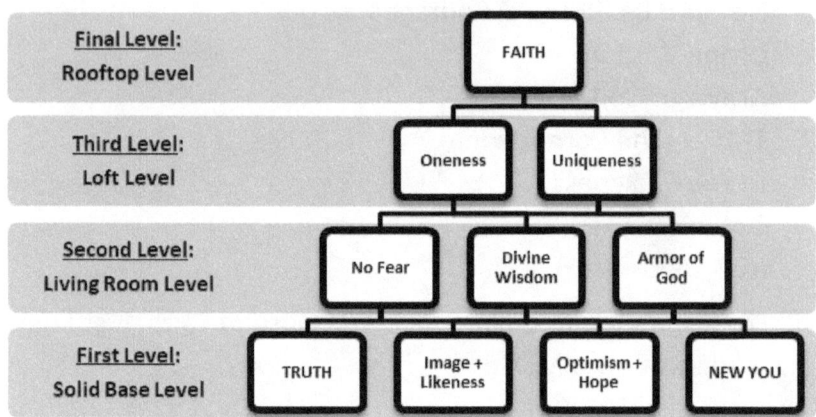

With this blueprint and framework, you are on your way to building your very own **House of Faith**.

HOW TO USE THIS BOOK

- **As a Handbook**: This book is your handbook and instruction manual to build your House of Faith and your roadmap on your inspirational journey. Here is a quick overview of how it's written:

  » **Block by Block.** Each building block reading section contains a **"Point to Ponder," "Words of Wisdom,"** and advice on **"Building by the Good Book"** (the "Good Book" is simply another way that some people refer to the Bible because of the good things that it can do for you when you read, learn, and apply God's Word to your life).

» **Builder Toolkit APPs.** At the end of each building block section, I also provide you with useful and practical daily tools for you to continue building your House of Faith and to learn more about that specific building block. These useful and practical tools are your "**Builder Toolkit APPs (Affirmation. Proactivity. Prayer).**"

In these APPs, I intentionally repeat certain general concepts that apply to each building block. For example, at the start of each **Affirmation**, I always say, "Affirm and activate [the specific building block] every day"; at the start of each **Proactivity**, I always say, "Be proactive and choose God's way every day"; and at the start of each **Prayer**, I always say, "Pray every day." It's important to hammer home these simple, general concepts as foundational practices and daily routines. I then follow up with Builder Toolkit APP information that is more specific to that particular building block.

» **The Power of Prayer.** In the **Prayer** part of the Builder Toolkit APPs, I provide you with a short, easy prayer to get you started talking with God about that specific topic (think of it as simply texting or chatting with Him). It's okay to not know how to pray. That's why Jesus taught us all how to pray with the simple but powerful Lord's Prayer found in Luke 11:2-4 and Matthew 6:9-13. And that's why I'm teaching you how to pray with each building block.

Prayer is powerful and transformational. It's also relational, not transactional. In other words, praying is about building a strong relationship with God. The goal isn't to check it off a to-do list. It's not like rubbing a magic lamp to get three wishes from a genie in a bottle, either.

Prayer transforms our hearts and minds in great ways. When we pray about something, we can see God's goodness in every outcome because of His presence, even if we don't receive the outcome we desire.

Pray always. It is your power source. The Good Book specifically says so! "...The earnest *prayer* of a righteous person *has great power and produces wonderful results*" (James 5:16, emphasis added).

- **From the Ground Up**: This book is intentionally written in a unique way: from the ground up. That means, even though the building blocks spell out the word F.O.U.N.D.A.T.I.O.N., we'll actually start at the bottom with "**N**" (NEW YOU) and work our way up each level to the top to "**F**" (FAITH). This is intentional. Remember, we are building a strong structure, and every building structure in history was built from the ground up!

- **Follow the Podcast**: To help you follow the book, I created The Found Boys companion podcast. You can follow it on Spotify, Apple, or wherever you listen to podcasts to make it part of your life and let it inspire and ignite you.

- **Be Flexible, Finish, and Share It**: As you read this book and apply its lessons, stay flexible. You don't have to read it all in one sitting.

You can read one building block per day as a 10-day challenge or read one per week as a 10-week challenge. Just stick with it. And if you put the book down for a while, that's okay! Just come back and finish. You've got this.

When you're finished, feel free to refer to this book often and go back and re-read any part of it anytime. You should even share it with others who can benefit from the valuable lessons you'll have learned.

- **Put It Into Practice:** Finally, this book is written as ten valuable life lessons in an acronym that spells the word F.O.U.N.D.A.T.I.O.N., but the life lessons don't need to be put into practice in real life in the exact order that they're written in this book.

   Also, as you'll see at the end of the book, three of the blocks — the "**T**" block (TRUTH), "**N**" block (NEW YOU), and "**F**" block (FAITH) — are connected in a 360 degree, synergistic way that aligns all of the other blocks in your House of Faith. This is intentional so you can see the cyclical nature of the framework. Other than that, you can apply the blocks in your life in any order. Basically, think of them like Legos: moveable and interchangeable building blocks that don't need to be placed in any particular order to build something awesome.

Your House of Faith construction project is simple but powerful. Just lay a solid F.O.U.N.D.A.T.I.O.N. for your life and level up your faith in God.

As you do, you (and your life) will transform in new and exciting ways... from a teen boy to a faithful, wise, and mighty young man. This is your Found Boy hero origin story.

So, let's GO... with GOD!

FIRST LEVEL:
THE SOLID BASE

The first level of your **F.O.U.N.D.A.T.I.O.N.** has four building blocks. These four blocks form the solid base of your House of Faith.

They ground you in your Faith.

Building Blocks for the First Level: The Solid Base

- **New You**

- **Optimism + Hope**

- **Image + Likeness**

- **Truth (The Cornerstone)**

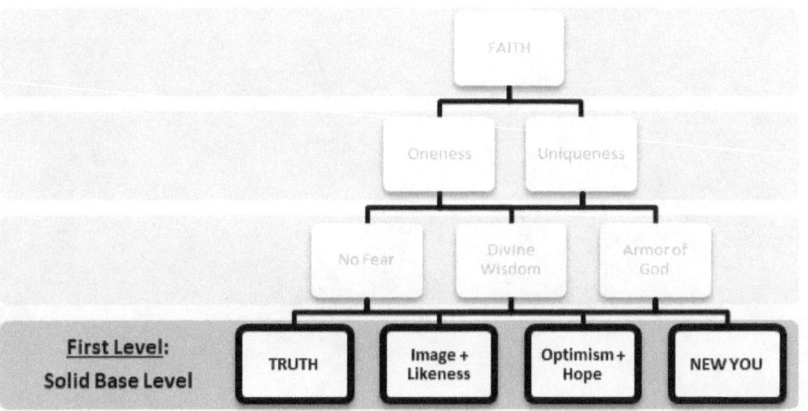

1

NEW YOU

• Point to Ponder •

Have you ever wondered what the best version of your unique life as a young man would look like? A greater and stronger "new you?"

Think about the following **Words of Wisdom**:

"Anyone who belongs to Christ has become a ***new person***. The old life is gone; ***a new life*** has begun!" (emphasis added)

Those wise words came from the New Testament: **2 Corinthians 5:17**, and they apply to your first building block for your House of Faith.

BUILDING BLOCK #1:
NEW YOU

The New You is part of a bigger blueprint and Master Plan, and God is the Master Builder.

The New You is a renovated and stronger version of you through faith in God. Jesus is the cornerstone in your House of Faith, and YOU are the other solid stone in the foundation. Your mission is to lay a solid foundation for your life by dedicating and connecting your whole self (including your thoughts, decisions, actions, and words) to the cornerstone, Jesus. When you do, you are on a journey of continuous improvement and renewal to become a new man, on a new level, in Christ: a new *you*.

As you take this life-giving journey to becoming a New You, you are building yourself into a faithful, wise, and mighty man of God. And remember, the Good Book (the Bible) is an excellent guidebook for your building project.

BUILDING BY THE GOOD BOOK

What does the Good Book say about the New You? It offers encouragement and advice for this new building block in your life by providing strength and support in the Word of God.

These powerful and inspirational verses will help you embrace a fresh new start in Jesus Christ:

- "Since you have heard about Jesus and have learned the truth that comes from him... let the Spirit ***renew your thoughts and attitudes***."

  —Ephesians 4:21-23 (emphasis added)

  » **How does this apply to you?** You might not know Jesus, or you might know very little about Jesus. When I was your age, I definitely knew less than I know now. Now that you are learning about Him, keep seeking and connecting with Him. As you do, your thoughts, attitudes, and nature will be renewed in positive and powerful ways through God.

- "Don't copy the behavior and customs of this world, but *let God transform you into a new person by changing the way you think*. Then you will learn to know God's will for you, which is good and pleasing and perfect."

  —Romans 12:2 (emphasis added)

  » **How does this apply to you?** Sometimes, it can be hard to hear God because worldly messages can be louder than His voice. But you can tune out the world and tune into God every day. One simple way to do this is to pray daily. It's also good to pray multiple times per day. For example, I often pray when I'm waking up, working out, listening to music, preparing meals for my teen kids, and going to bed. Prayer is simply talking to God. You don't have to always be on your knees to pray. Sometimes you have a lot to say, and sometimes you have little to say. Either way, God loves it when you talk to Him. As you do, you will become better at knowing God's good will for your unique life, and He will transform you into a new person: the best and greatest version of *you*!

- "But to all who *believed him and accepted him*, he gave the right to become children of God. They are *reborn* — not with a physical birth resulting from human passion or plan, but *a birth that comes from God*."

  —John 1:12-13 (emphasis added)

- **How does this apply to you?** "Believe" and "accept" are two simple but powerful words. Think about all of the little things you believe and accept on a daily basis. You might believe and accept what you saw on social media today, what your friend told you today, or what your teacher taught you in school this week. But what if you believed and accepted the best thing you could ever imagine for your life? By believing and accepting Jesus, you are re-born and become a child of the Most High God. Simply put, you become a new and improved version of *you*.

These are just a few verses in the Good Book that will help you live by faith and trust in God at all times through the ups and downs in life. As you continue to grow in your faith, there are many more that you will learn along the way.

Here are some practical tools for you to continue building your House of Faith and to help you apply the New You building block to your life.

BUILDER TOOLKIT APP
(AFFIRMATION. PROACTIVITY. PRAYER.)

AFFIRMATION:

Affirm and activate the New You. One simple way is to say this easy, powerful phrase to yourself every day:

"I am new. I am reborn. I am transforming into a better person by changing the way I think and live."

Ask God every day to help you align your affirmations and actions with His perfect plans for your life.

PROACTIVITY:

Be proactive and choose God's way every day.

You can know God's way through praying, reading the Good Book, and learning from other Christians. Be prepared, set goals, and pursue the plans that God reveals to you through these ways.

Stay positive and make progress on your new journey and mission of continuous improvement and renewal to become the New You. To help you, just know:

- **You matter to God.** God loves you, understands you, and cares for you.

- **You are unique.** God gave you special gifts and talents. Maybe you're good at academics, sports, music, languages, or fixing and building things... Whatever it is, you have unique God-given gifts and talents. Oftentimes, God has blessed you to be good at multiple things.

- **You were created for a purpose.** God wants you to use your gifts and talents for good. As you find and fulfill that God-given purpose, you become the New You: the faithful, wise, and mighty young man you were created and intended to be.

• Prayer •

Pray every day.

Ask God to guide you in all of your thoughts, decisions, actions, and words.

Use this short, simple prayer anytime to start an open and honest chat with God about the New You:

"Father God, it's me, [your name].

Thank You for caring about me, understanding me, and loving me. Thank you for blessing me with the opportunity to learn about Jesus and Your truth. I want to know Your good and perfect will for my life. Please renew my thoughts and attitudes and transform me into a new person as I get to know You and become more like You.

In Jesus's name, Amen."

2

OPTIMISM + HOPE

~~~

• Point to Ponder •

Have you ever wanted to improve your strength, courage, and endurance to overcome obstacles in your life? That power and optimism in you to overcome obstacles is called *hope*.

Think about the following **Words of Wisdom**:

"We rejoice in *hope* of the glory of God. Not only that, but we rejoice in our sufferings, knowing that suffering produces endurance, and endurance produces character, and character produces *hope*..." (emphasis added)

Those wise words came from the New Testament: **Romans 5:2-4, ESV**, and they apply to your second building block for your House of Faith.

BUILDING BLOCK #2:
OPTIMISM + HOPE

As a teen, one of my favorite movies was Star Wars: Episode IV: A New Hope.[1] In one particular scene, as Princess Leia is being chased down by Darth Vader, she sends a message to her older Jedi friend. We later learn the message said, "Help me, Obi-Wan Kenobi. You're our only hope." That's one of my favorite movie lines, and I always imagined myself being a hero like Obi-Wan and protecting people. I wanted people to have hope in me, and I still do. As humans, we can all certainly do good and heroic things in the world to help other people. God will honor that lifestyle, but God is the ultimate source of hope, not us.

Before we dive into our life lesson on this building block, allow me to clarify one thing about optimism and hope: they are similar, but there are differences. Hope is greater than optimism because hope is found in God, and it is a firm and steady force. Optimism is good, but it can be fleeting and wavering, depending on your view of the world. For example, many people say, "An optimist sees a glass as half full, while a pessimist sees a glass as half empty." So, while it's better to be an optimist than a pessimist, having HOPE is better than both.

The good news is that you can combine worldly optimism with heavenly hope. Our goal is to have optimism in the world *and* hope in God.

Sometimes in life, you face troubles and storms that threaten to shatter your dreams. That certainly happened to me when I flunked out of college and then later when I lost my job as a lawyer several times.

---

[1] Lucas, George, director. Star Wars: Episode IV: A New Hope. Lucasfilm, 1977.

But you have a choice. You have the freedom to choose how you will respond to trouble and storms. You can choose to be optimistic or pessimistic; you can choose hope or despair. Choose optimism and hope. When you choose to have hope in God in the midst of hard times, you can experience the fullness of joy in life.

And when troubles and storms arise, it's okay to experience every emotion and pour them out in a healthy way: walk, run, lift, hunt, build, cook, write, draw, sing, dance, code, play, or do your favorite healthy thing, whatever it is. But in the end, you should always have hope and look to God in the middle of those troubles – not because you're happy (it's okay and healthy to be sad when bad things happen), but because you know God is in the middle of the storm with you.

God will never leave you. No matter what dreams are broken, what troubles arise, or what storms of life may come. Jesus said, "...In this world, you will have trouble. But take heart! I have overcome the world" (John 16:33, NIV). Jesus is essentially saying, "The world is full of storms, but *have hope*. I will protect you and carry you through the storm." No matter what you face, Jesus will help you overcome it. So, choose to recognize God's presence and power in all circumstances. Choosing God is choosing optimism and *hope*.

BUILDING BY THE GOOD BOOK

What does the Good Book say about optimism and hope? It offers encouragement and advice for this new building block in your life by providing strength and support in the Word of God.

These powerful and inspirational verses will help you over-flow and rejoice with optimism and hope in all circumstances through Jesus Christ:

- "I pray that God, *the source of hope*, will fill you comple-tely with joy and peace because you trust in him. Then *you will overflow with confident hope* through the power of the Holy Spirit."
  —Romans 15:13 (emphasis added)

  » **How does this apply to you?** God is the source of hope, and you can always count on Him. He will always help you and protect you. If you're not seeing God's protec-tion right now, then pray and ask Him to reveal more of His plans to you, and then look in places where you might not usually look. The more you trust Him, the more you will overflow with confidence, joy, and peace.

- "And his name will be *the hope of all the world*."
  —Matthew 12:21 (emphasis added)

  » **How does this apply to you?** God sent His one and only son, Jesus, not to judge the world but to save the world (John 3:17), overcome the world (John 16:33), and be the hope of the world (Matthew 12:21). God sent Je-sus to save you, not judge you, no matter what mistakes you might've made. God also sent Jesus to overcome the brokenness you might experience in the world and be your hope and light in times of darkness.

- "Instead, you must worship Christ as Lord of your life. And if someone asks about *your hope as a believer*, always be ready to explain it."
  —1 Peter 3:15 (emphasis added)

» **How does this apply to you?** When you believe and put your hope in God, you are saved and can overcome any obstacle. Jesus specifically said, "If you remain in me and my words remain in you, ask whatever you wish, and it will be done for you" (John 15:7, NIV). Jesus is the faithful, wise, and mighty name you should always call upon, not as a magic genie to grant your wishes but as a savior to answer your prayers. His answer is often yes, no, or not yet, so sometimes you have to be patient with your requests and seek alignment with God through your faith.

Jesus's disciple John said it this way: "This is the confidence we have in approaching God: that *if we ask anything according to His will, He hears us*" (1 John 5:14, NIV; emphasis added). And the apostle Paul said it this way: "Rejoice in our *confident hope*. Be patient in trouble, and keep on praying" (Romans 12:12; emphasis added). Through Jesus, we know that God hears us as we trust Him with our prayers. So, any time someone asks you about your hope in God through Jesus, you have a great opportunity to share your faith with genuine joy.

These are just a few verses in the Good Book that will help you live by faith and trust in God at all times through the ups and downs in life. As you continue to grow in your faith, there are many more that you will learn along the way.

Here are some practical tools for you to continue building your House of Faith and to help you apply the Optimism + Hope building block to your life.

BUILDER TOOLKIT APP
(AFFIRMATION. PROACTIVITY. PRAYER.)

AFFIRMATION:

Affirm and activate your optimism and hope in God. One simple way is to say this easy, powerful phrase to yourself every day:

> **"I am overflowing with optimism and hope. I trust in God, the true source of hope. I am full of confidence, joy, and peace in every situation."**

Ask God every day to help you align your affirmations and actions with His perfect plans for your life.

PROACTIVITY:

Be proactive and choose God's way every day.

You can know God's way through praying, reading the Good Book, and learning from other Christians. Be prepared, set goals, and pursue the plans that God reveals to you through these ways.

Stay positive and make progress on your new journey and mission of continuous improvement and renewal to be full of joy and overflow with optimism and hope. Have high hopes for the goals you want to achieve to help you get ahead and overcome obstacles in your life:

- **Pen**: Write down 2-3 goals that you want to accomplish this month or this year.

- **Post**: Then, post them where you will see them every day.

- **Push**: Finally, push through. When you see your written goals, read them out loud and remind yourself what you are working towards. And remember, that power and optimism in you to overcome obstacles is called *hope*. Find the strength through Christ to persevere in both good and hard times.

Prayer

Pray every day.

Ask God to guide you in all of your thoughts, decisions, actions, and words.

Use this short, simple prayer anytime to start an open and honest chat with God about optimism and hope:

ಜಿ

"Father God, it's me, [your name].

Thank You for being the source of hope. I want to overflow with confident hope through Your power. When I face troubles and the storms of life, help me to turn toward You and not away from You. Help me to remember in those hard times that You are always with me and that by choosing You, I can choose joy and peace. Please fill me completely with joy and peace because I trust in You.

In Jesus's name, Amen."

3

IMAGE + LIKENESS

~~~

• Point to Ponder •

Have you ever wanted to be like your favorite athlete, music star, entrepreneur, or social media influencer?

What if I told you that you were born in the *image and likeness* of the undisputed Greatest of All Time (and I'm not talking about LeBron James, Tom Brady, Mr. Beast, or any other famous person that the world refers to as the "GOAT").

Think about the following **Words of Wisdom**:

"Then God said, 'Let us make human beings *in our image to be like us*...' So God created human beings *in his own image. In the image of God he created them*; male and female he created them. Then God blessed them..." (emphasis added)

Those wise words came from the **Book of Genesis 1:26-28,** and they apply to your third building block for your House of Faith.

BUILDING BLOCK #3:
IMAGE + LIKENESS

As you now know, I'm talking about God. The Book of Genesis specifically says that God created humans in His image and likeness. And then guess what? He blessed them. God is so good.

To help you understand how this applies to you, let's go back to the very first building block. Remember? You learned about the New You.

When the world is telling you that you're a mistake, that you're not worthy or good enough, do NOT believe that lie. Instead, pause and remember the truth. You are a masterpiece. A valuable work of art that God thoughtfully designed. That is your true identity. Allow that truth to inform your thoughts and decisions throughout each and every day.

As an African-American teen growing up in a poor part of Florida, I never knew any lawyers or authors that looked like me or were from my part of the world. The world was telling me, and other teen guys like me, that I should be doing drugs, committing crimes, or in a grave. But through my faith, education, and work ethic, I became exactly what God truly intended me to be in my life: a strong Christian attorney and author, a loving family man, and a good dad. That's my true identity, and God can help you discover yours.

BUILDING BY THE GOOD BOOK

What does the Good Book say about you being created in God's image and likeness? It offers encouragement and advice for this new building block in your life by providing strength and support in the Word of God.

These powerful and inspirational verses will help you to know that you are intentionally created in God's image and likeness:

- "For *we are God's masterpiece. He has created us anew in Christ Jesus*, so we can do the good things he planned for us long ago."

  —Ephesians 2:10 (emphasis added)

  » **How does this apply to you?** You are God's *masterpiece*, and He has good things in store for you and your life. He has created you anew in Jesus, and you can do all things through Jesus who strengthens you (Philippians 4:13).

- "Put on your new nature, *created to be like God* — truly righteous and holy."

  —Ephesians 4:24 (emphasis added)

  » **How does this apply to you?** As you work towards the New You, remember that we were all created to be like God. As humans, none of us can be exactly like God. However, He still wants us to work toward His standard. He wants us to truly live right in His sight and receive His blessings. Nobody is perfect except Jesus. God knows that we're not perfect and still cares for us. He wants you to always pursue the New You.

- "Put on your new nature, and be renewed as you *learn to know your Creator and become like Him*."

  —Colossians 3:10 (emphasis added)

» **How does this apply to you?** Similar to the verse above in Ephesians, we're called to put on our new nature. As you go through this powerful renewal process with God through Jesus Christ, you will learn to know your Creator better, gain divine wisdom, and become more like Him.

You might notice similarities between this Image + Likeness building block and the New You building block. That's good because these concepts are meant to align and piece together within your House of Faith framework.

These are just a few verses in the Good Book that will help you live by faith and trust in God at all times through the ups and downs in life. As you continue to grow in your faith, there are many more that you will learn along the way.

Here are some practical tools for you to continue building your House of Faith and to help you apply the Image + Likeness building block to your life.

BUILDER TOOLKIT APP
(AFFIRMATION. PROACTIVITY. PRAYER.)

AFFIRMATION:

Affirm that you were created in God's image and likeness. One simple way is to say this easy, powerful phrase to yourself every day:

"I am God's masterpiece, created in His image and likeness. I will do the good things that He has planned

for me. I am becoming the best version of the man that God created and intended me to be."

Ask God every day to help you align your affirmations and actions with His perfect plans for your life.

PROACTIVITY:

Be proactive and choose God's way every day.

You can know God's way through praying, reading the Good Book, and learning from other Christians. Be prepared, set goals, and pursue the plans that God reveals to you through these ways.

Stay positive and make progress on your new journey and mission of continuous improvement and renewal to understand the power and joy of being made in God's image and likeness. To help you, just discover and remember your true identity:

- God made you in His image to be like Him. Truly good, just like God. You are a son of the Most High God. That is your true identity.

- God blessed you when He created you. He gave you gifts and purposes that are unique to you. God is the undisputed G.O.A.T. (Greatest of All Time), and we are His S.H.E.E.P. (Serving His Eternal & Everlasting Purposes).

- God gave you power to use your unique gifts and purpose to do good things on this earth. Think about that... God empowers you to partner with Him in blessing other people on earth!

• Prayer •

Pray every day.

Ask God to guide you in all of your thoughts, decisions, actions, and words.

Use this short, simple prayer anytime to start an open and honest chat with God about His image and likeness:

"Father God, it's me, [your name].

Thank You for carefully creating me in Your image and likeness. I want to do the good things You have planned for my life. Please show me my true identity in You and help me to see myself the way that You see me, as Your unique masterpiece.

In Jesus's name, Amen."

4

TRUTH
(THE CORNERSTONE)

~~~

• Point to Ponder •

At the beginning of this book, I asked you an important question about truth:

"What if someone told you the truth about who you are?"

In this chapter, let's dig deeper: what if someone shared the truth with you about **HOW** to live your best life ever?

Think about the following **Words of Wisdom**:

"Jesus said to the people who believed in him, 'You are truly my disciples if you remain faithful to my teachings. And you will know *the truth*, and **the *truth*** will set you free.'" (emphasis added)

Those wise words came from the New Testament: **John 8:31-32**, and they apply to your cornerstone building block for your House of Faith.

BUILDING BLOCK - THE CORNERSTONE:
TRUTH

Jesus Christ is the Truth. He is the Cornerstone and the very first block to be laid down in your House of Faith. Did you know that in every building project, the builders lay down the cornerstone first because it is used to align all of the other blocks in that particular building? In the same way, Jesus is the Cornerstone that aligns all other building blocks in your House of Faith. It all starts with Him.

Jesus is the way, the truth, and the life (John 14:6). He is also one of the Holy Trinity: God the Father, Jesus Christ the Son of God, and the Holy Spirit (Matthew 28:19).

The Truth is that God loves you so much that He sent His one and only Son, Jesus, to save you and give you eternal life. One of Jesus's greatest followers, John, put it this way:

> "Dear friends, let us continue to **love one another**, for **love comes from God**. Anyone who loves is a child of God and knows God. But anyone who does not love does not know God, for **God is love. God showed how much He loved us by sending His one and only Son into the world so that we might have eternal life through Him. This is real love...**"
>
> —1 John 4:7-10, emphasis added

In other words, Jesus loves you, calls you by name, and improves your life eternally when you accept and follow Him. And when you experience life eternally with Jesus, you're called to share this Good News with others to help lead them to Jesus so they can benefit, too!

Simply put, Jesus Christ is the Truth about how to live your best life ever. So, live, love, and lead like Jesus.

BUILDING BY THE GOOD BOOK

What does the Good Book say about the Truth? It offers encouragement and advice for this new building block in your life by providing strength and support in the Word of God.

These powerful and inspirational verses will help you know that Jesus Christ is the Truth and the Cornerstone of our lives:

- "...I am the way, *the truth*, and the life. No one can come to the Father except through me."

  —John 14:6 (emphasis added)

  » **How does this apply to you?** To help you understand what Jesus is saying in this verse, here's more background on why he said it. Before Jesus said these specific words, a young man named Thomas was feeling lost and having trouble trusting in God and finding his way (sounds familiar, right?). Well, this young guy is often called "Doubting Thomas" and was actually one of Jesus's disciples. And at one point, when Jesus explains to His disciples that He must leave to prepare a place in His Father's House for those who believe in Him, Thomas doubts and questions Jesus by adamantly stating, "We have no idea where you are going, so how can we know the way?" Jesus responded, "*I AM* the *Way*, the *Truth*, and the *Life*. No one can come to the Father except through me" (John 14:6, emphasis added).

  You see, Jesus shared the *truth* about His identity with honesty and clear authority. He expressed His love for

Thomas and all of His disciples and everyone in the world, including you and me. He shared the truth about how to live our best life ever.

- "Those who speak on their own seek glory for themselves. Those who seek the glory of him who sent me are people of **truth**; there's no falsehood in them."

—John 7:18, CEB (emphasis added)

» **How does this apply to you?** You can live your best life ever by seeking the glory of God. It's okay to have ambition and seek to achieve great things in life. Just ask God to make sure your goals and desires are in alignment with His truths and good plans for your life.

For example, if you pray to God to someday be rich and famous, you should also be clear in your heart and prayers about your motives. If you're praying for this as a means to support yourself and your family or to help others with your fame and wealth, then you're likely seeking it for good reasons that align with God's plans and glory. But if you're praying for it to be greedy and show off to others, then you're likely seeking it for the wrong reasons and your own selfish glory.

- "Jesus said to them, 'Have you never read in the Scriptures: 'The stone that the builders rejected has become **the cornerstone**; this was the Lord's doing, and it is marvelous in our eyes'?'"

—Matthew 21:42, ESV (emphasis added)

» **How does this apply to you?** As you learned earlier in the first building block, your mission for your House of

Faith is to create a solid foundation for your life by connecting yourself to the cornerstone, Jesus. Pray, read the Good Book, and connect with other solid Christians. When you do, you are on a journey of continuous improvement and renewal to become a new man on a new level in Christ... a New You.

Peter said it this way: "You are coming to Christ, who is **the living cornerstone** of God's temple. He was rejected by people, but he was chosen by God for great honor. And **you are living stones** that God is building into his spiritual temple..." (1 Peter 2:4-5, emphasis added).

And Paul said it this way: "**Together, we are his house, built on the foundation** of the apostles and the prophets. **And the cornerstone is Christ Jesus himself**" (Ephesians 2:20, emphasis added). As you come to Jesus, the cornerstone, and build your own "House of Faith," you are a living stone being built into God's house: the spiritual temple of God's global church.

These are just a few verses in the Good Book that will help you live by faith and trust in God at all times through the ups and downs in life. As you continue to grow in your faith, there are many more that you will learn along the way.

Here are some practical tools for you to continue building your House of Faith and to help you apply the Truth building block to your life.

BUILDER TOOLKIT APP
(AFFIRMATION. PROACTIVITY. PRAYER.)

AFFIRMATION:

Affirm and activate the Truth. One simple way is to say this easy, powerful phrase to yourself every day:

> **"I believe the Truth. I am a living stone, and I am aligning my life with the Cornerstone, Jesus Christ. Each day, I live, love, and lead like Jesus."**

Ask God every day to help you align your affirmations and actions with His perfect plans for your life.

PROACTIVITY:

Be proactive and choose God's way every day.

You can know God's way through praying, reading the Good Book, and learning from other Christians. Be prepared, set goals, and pursue the plans that God reveals to you through these ways.

Stay positive and make progress on your new journey and mission of continuous improvement and renewal to learn and understand the truth that comes from Jesus. Always choose truth:

- Truth is the cornerstone and foundation of Faith. As you build the foundation for your life, start with God's Word.

- Truth defeats lies. God is the source of truth, and on the flip side, there's an enemy roaming this world that is the source of lies (referred to in the Bible as the devil or sa-tan). Always choose truth; never choose lies. Win with the truth and defeat the enemy's lies. Every lie has a negative impact on your life.

- Truth frees you to grow in great ways. It frees you from mistakes, wrong choices, and the burden of carrying lies. Truth frees you to have strength and courage during hard times. Most importantly, every truth has a positive impact on your life.

• Prayer •

Pray every day.

Ask God to guide you in all of your thoughts, decisions, actions, and words.

Use this short, simple prayer anytime to start an open and honest chat with God about the Truth:

૱

"Father God, it's me, [your name].

Thank You for the truth that comes from Jesus, the Cornerstone. I want to learn and live the truth and be aligned with You. Please help me to always choose truth; never choose lies. Please help me to win with the truth, and defeat the enemy's lies. Please allow the truth of Your Word to change my life and transform me and others around me. Please help me bring the people I know to faith in Christ and to the knowledge and acceptance of His truth. Help me to become a faithful, wise, and mighty young man of God founded by YOUR TRUTH.

In Jesus's name, Amen."

SECOND LEVEL:
THE LIVING ROOM

~~~

The second level of your **F.O.U.N.D.A.T.I.O.N.** has three building blocks. These three blocks form the living room for your House of Faith.

They help you live out your life on a daily basis in Faith.

Building Blocks for the Second Level: The Living Room

- **Armor of God**

- **Divine Wisdom**

- **No Fear: Be Strong + Courageous**

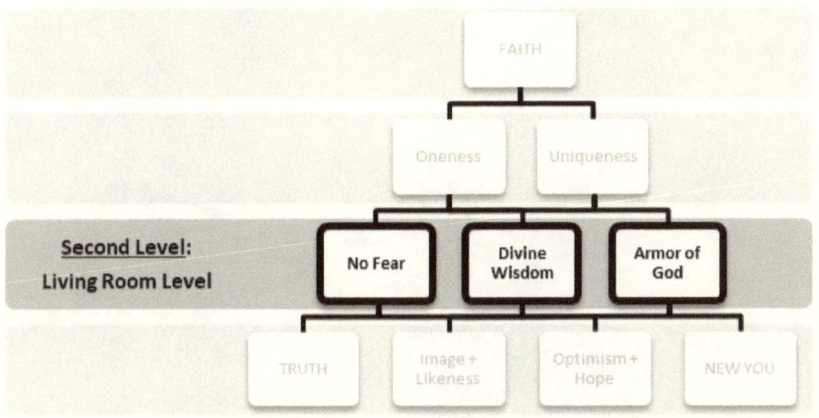

5

ARMOR OF GOD

~~~

• Point to Ponder •

Imagine you're a doctor, and you need to save a life by performing emergency surgery. Would you do it without a medical mask, surgical scrubs, and gloves?

Or what if you were a firefighter? Would you run into a burning building without a gas mask, protective helmet, and fireproof suit?

Or better yet, how about a soldier? (I know you've played Call Of Duty, Halo, or Fortnite!) Would you head into battle without the best body armor and weapons you can get?

Nope! In all three situations, you would gear up in *full armor*. In fact, not only would you gear up, but you would also spend years preparing for these dangerous jobs and learning to protect yourself from harm!

So, how does this apply to you today? Since the beginning of time, humans have been a target of the devil, and he's always trying to draw the world away from God and destroy God's children. Well, *God loves us so much that he even taught us how to fight the enemy.*

Love God. Love people. Fight the devil. I'm pumped, are you?? Let's go... with GOD!!!

Think about the following **Words of Wisdom**:

"Finally, be strong in the Lord and in his mighty power. Put on **the full armor of God**, so that you can take your stand against the devil's schemes." (emphasis added)

Those wise words came from the New Testament: **Ephesians 6:10-11, NIV**, and they apply to your fifth building block for your House of Faith.

BUILDING BLOCK #5:
ARMOR OF GOD

Every day, you face spiritual battles that you cannot fully see. The devil will attack and try to get you to believe lies about God, your situation, yourself, or other people to achieve his evil schemes and plans. He will try to get you to doubt your God-given authority and true identity.

But God is always fighting for you and gives you victory over this enemy. When you have faith and accept Jesus, you join His team, and He gives you the spiritual Armor to win with the Truth and defeat the enemy's lies.

So, what does this Armor consist of? Here are the six powerful pieces of the Armor of God for you to gear up with:

ARMOR ITEM #1: YOUR BELT - TRUTH

Always look to God's definition of Truth. As we learned in our last building block, Truth can be found in Jesus: He is the Way, the Truth, and the Life.

It is the Truth of Jesus that holds everything together, just like a belt does.

Every day, put on your Belt of TRUTH. One simple way to do this is to learn more about Jesus and follow His teachings in the Good Book.

ARMOR ITEM #2: YOUR BREASTPLATE - RIGHTEOUSNESS

Righteousness means living in alignment with God: His will, His words, and His way of life. When we follow God faithfully in this way, we are living according to His design for our life. This right living is a covering for us in spiritual battles: it is a breastplate.

A breastplate is basically a bulletproof vest. It protects the wearer's heart, lungs, and other internal organs. If the enemy tries to land a fatal blow by attacking us, righteousness protects us every time by covering us as we "stand right" with Jesus.

Every day, put on your Breastplate of RIGHTEOUSNESS. One simple way to do this is to do good when you're faced with the temptation to do something bad. Think of it this way: temptation is simply the opportunity to do the right thing. Ask yourself, "What would Jesus do?"

ARMOR ITEM # 3: YOUR SHOES - PEACE

Jesus is often called the "Prince of Peace." As He was approaching His final days in the world, He said that He was leaving us with a gift – peace of mind and heart. This peace comes from accepting Jesus and receiving the gift of the Holy Spirit inside of us. It's a powerful peace that comes from faith in God; it's not something we can get from the world around us. God's peace exceeds anything we can understand and guards our hearts and minds as we live in alignment with Jesus (Philippians 4:7).

Your Shoes of Peace are your battle boots. Just as the right shoes can provide solid ground and stable footing on treacherous terrain, the right spiritual shoes can help you stand firm and confident in the spiritual battles you face when the enemy attacks.

Every day, put on your Shoes of PEACE. One simple way to do this is to pray to God for His perfect peace in the midst of a hard situation and be proactive. Be a part of the solution instead of being reactive and contributing to the chaos and the problem.

ARMOR ITEM # 4: YOUR SHIELD - FAITH

We are saved by faith in Jesus Christ. We can defend ourselves again and again by choosing to trust in Him and His Truth rather than the lies of the enemy.

Your Shield of Faith not only stops the enemy's fiery arrows and bullets but also extinguishes them. When attacks like anxiety, disappointment, fear, or depression come whizzing toward you, faith helps you stop those negative thoughts, overcome them, and press forward. Arrow by arrow and bullet by bullet, you overcome the enemy's lies by choosing to trust in God's truth instead. If the enemy tries to tell you that you're not good at school, trust in God's truth about your academic ability. If the enemy tries to tell you that you're too nerdy to fit in, trust in God's truth about your ability to build a cool community of friends. Most importantly, have faith in God's good plans for your life.

Every day, raise your Shield of FAITH. One simple way to do this is to choose to get better, not bitter. In the face of adversity, know that your faith in God will help you overcome. Through your faith, you will never lose; you will either win or learn.

ARMOR ITEM # 5: YOUR HELMET - SALVATION

Salvation means being saved and protected from evil, harm, and sin. Salvation comes through Jesus Christ alone, and nothing can separate us from Him. So when we trust in Him for salvation, our souls are protected, and our eternity is secure.

One of the enemy's most effective weapons against us is discouragement. The devil wants you to give up and give in to his evil plans. Your Helmet of Salvation gives you the assurance that God will help you defeat the devil, and it protects you against the desire to give up and give in. When you are properly equipped with the Helmet of Salvation, you have hope. You stay in the fight, marching toward victory, and you don't give up.

Every day, put on your Helmet of SALVATION. One simple way to do this is to accept Jesus in your heart as your Lord and Savior, and when things get so hard that you want to give up and give in, then get down on your knees, pray, and praise the Lord. He who kneels before God can stand before anyone!

FINALLY, ARMOR ITEM # 6: YOUR SWORD - SPIRIT (THE WORD OF GOD)

The Sword of the Spirit is the Word of God. To effectively use the sword, we have to know and follow God's Word.

If you can bring only one weapon into battle, bring the Sword of the Spirit, which can be used both defensively and offensively. You can wield this sword by memorizing God's Word and applying its teachings. When you know what God's Word says, you can use it defensively to confidently deflect the lies the devil tries to tell you, and you can use it offensively as a powerful light to give hope to others and do good in the world.

Every day, wield your Sword of the SPIRIT. One simple way to do this is to memorize and internalize your favorite verses from the Good Book daily. Some people call these "life verses."

BUILDING BY THE GOOD BOOK

What does the Good Book say about the Armor of God? It offers encouragement and advice for this new building block in your life by providing strength and support in the Word of God.

This single, powerful, and inspirational verse will help you put on the full Armor of God:

- "A final word: Be strong in the Lord and in his mighty power. Put on **all of God's armor** so that you will be able to stand firm against all strategies of the devil. For we are not fighting against flesh-and-blood enemies, but against evil rulers and authorities of the unseen world, against mighty powers in this dark world, and against evil spirits in the heavenly places. Therefore, put on **every piece of**

God's armor so you will be able to resist the enemy in the time of evil. Then after the battle you will still be standing firm. Stand your ground, putting on the belt of truth and the body armor of God's righteousness. For shoes, put on the peace that comes from the Good News so that you will be fully prepared. In addition to all of these, hold up the shield of faith to stop the fiery arrows of the devil. Put on salvation as your helmet, and take the sword of the Spirit, which is the word of God. Pray in the Spirit at all times and on every occasion. Stay alert and be persistent in your prayers for all believers everywhere."

—Ephesians 6:10-18 (emphasis added)

» **How does this apply to you?** We can withstand any spiritual attack because of who we stand with: Jesus Christ. It is the Armor of God — Faith in Him and His Truth, Righteousness, Peace, and Salvation — which we wear. He has given us all the protective gear we need with one notable offensive weapon: the Sword of the Spirit. When you intentionally put on the full Armor of God, you can be ready for the enemy's attacks that will inevitably come your way.

This is one of many verses that will help you live by faith and trust in God at all times through the ups and downs in life. As you continue to grow in your faith, there are many more that you will learn along the way.

Here are some practical tools for you to continue building your House of Faith and to help you apply the Armor of God building block to your life.

BUILDER TOOLKIT APP (AFFIRMATION. PROACTIVITY. PRAYER.)

AFFIRMATION:

Affirm and activate the full Armor of God. One simple way is to say this easy, powerful phrase to yourself every day:

"I put on the full armor of God and stand my ground with Him by my side. I win with the Truth and defeat the enemy's lies. Through God's power, I am more than a conqueror."

Ask God every day to help you align your affirmations and actions with His perfect plans for your life.

PROACTIVITY:

Be proactive and choose God's way every day.

You can know God's way through praying, reading the Good Book, and learning from other Christians. Be prepared, set goals, and pursue the plans that God reveals to you through these ways.

Stay positive and make progress on your new journey and mission of continuous improvement and renewal to put on the full Armor of God. To help you, just remember to gear up and stand strong:

- God graciously gives us armor so that when we experience a spiritual attack, we will stand strong and fight by His strength.

- God has given you a call, a mission, a course to fulfill in life. The devil will do his best to stop it. When he attacks and intimidates, you are to stand strong in God's protective armor.

- Know that no matter what you face, God is already fighting for you. He is in control, and He will never leave you. He will never let you fall as long as you keep walking with Him. When you belong to God, you have the power to subdue, crush, and overthrow anything the devil throws at you. God's power makes you more than a conqueror.

• Prayer •

Pray every day.

Ask God to guide you in all of your thoughts, decisions, actions, and words.

Use this short, simple prayer anytime to start an open and honest chat with God about the Armor of God:

ೞ

"Father God, it's me, [your name].

Thank You for loving me so much that You protect me and teach me how to put on Your full Armor and fight the enemy. I want to fill my mind with truth, hold fast to my faith, guard my heart, walk in peace toward people, and understand Your Word so I can wield it as a weapon against any spiritual attack from the enemy that comes my way. Please help me put on the full Armor of God every day. I know that You will help me endure and remain resilient in the face of spiritual battles and tough times. With You, I am more than a conqueror.

In Jesus's name, Amen."

6

DIVINE WISDOM

~~~

• Point to Ponder •

When you want to learn something, where do you go to get started? Do you check out YouTube, Google, TikTok, or Instagram? You probably look for an influencer or expert to give you information or explanation on how to do that exact thing you want to learn.

In fact, the world is full of ways to gain knowledge and become smarter. You can learn from the internet, schools, books, or other sources.

But what if I told you that there's an ultimate and un-limited source of *wisdom*, knowledge, and understanding? And if you go to that source, you can learn to build your best life ever?

Well, since we're already talking about wisdom, I won't keep you in suspense! Think about the following **Words of Wisdom**:

"Anyone who listens to my teaching and follows it is *wise*, like a person who *builds a house on solid rock*." (emphasis added)

Those wise words came from the New Testament, **Matthew 7:24**, and they apply to your sixth building block for your House of Faith.

BUILDING BLOCK #6:
DIVINE WISDOM

You guessed it. The ultimate influencer and expert is Jesus. That's Jesus talking above, and in this verse, He explains another building block in your House of Faith: God's wisdom. Wisdom is knowledge, intuition, and experience combined to guide us in our thoughts and actions.

God's wisdom is perfect in knowledge and truth because God made the world and everything in it. He knows how life works best, so true wisdom – divine wisdom – comes from God (not the world or other humans). Unfortunately, we often look to the world, ourselves, or others to tell us who we are, what to think, and how life works, but as you know, the world and people are not perfect.

Jesus said it this way: "Seek the Kingdom of God above all else, and live righteously, and he will give you everything you need" (Matthew 6:33).

Just like the other building blocks you're learning about in this book, divine wisdom starts with a God-centered foundation. Everything else is built on that rock. Block by block, with Jesus as your rock, you can build and establish a supremely strong structure for your life: a House of Faith.

BUILDING BY THE GOOD BOOK

What does the Good Book say about divine wisdom? It offers encouragement and advice for this new building block in your life by providing strength and support in the Word of God.

These powerful and inspirational verses will help you seek, gain, and apply divine wisdom through Jesus Christ:

- "If you need **wisdom**, ask our generous God, and he will give it to you. He will not rebuke you for asking. But when you ask him, be sure that your **faith** is in God alone. Do not waver, for a person with divided loyalty is as unsettled as a wave of the sea that is blown and tossed by the wind."
  —James 1:5-6 (emphasis added)

  » **How does this apply to you?** Divine wisdom is a gift from God. You always have free and easy access to God's wisdom… simply look to Him and study His ways. God gives His wisdom freely and generously. You can and should ask God for wisdom.

- "If you are **wise** and understand God's ways, prove it by living an honorable life, **doing good works** with the humility that comes from **wisdom**."
  —James 3:13 (emphasis added)

  » **How does this apply to you?** Divine wisdom is intended to be used. Don't just learn it and sit on it. When God gives you wisdom, do good works with it. Act on it and apply it in your life with humility. When you live with divine wisdom, you will be a bright light for God in this world.

- "I want them to be encouraged and knit together by strong ties of love. I want them to have complete confidence that they **understand God's mysterious plan, which is Christ himself. In him lie hidden the treasures of wisdom and knowledge**."
  —Colossians 2:2-3 (emphasis added)

» **How does this apply to you?** As you seek divine wisdom, you become a treasure hunter. Divine wisdom is so valuable from God's eternal perspective that it is hidden like a treasure, only to be found through Jesus Christ himself, the ultimate influencer and expert on life. Once you find and gain this hidden treasure and ultimate source of knowledge, you begin to understand and have complete confidence in God's plan for your life.

These are just a few verses in the Good Book that will help you live by faith and trust in God at all times through the ups and downs in life. As you continue to grow in your faith, there are many more that you will learn along the way.

Here are some practical tools for you to continue building your House of Faith and to help you apply the Divine Wisdom building block to your life.

BUILDER TOOLKIT APP
(AFFIRMATION. PROACTIVITY. PRAYER.)

AFFIRMATION:

Affirm and activate divine wisdom. One simple way is to say this easy, powerful phrase to yourself every day:

"I seek God's wisdom and apply it to my life. With this divine wisdom, I do good works in the world. And even on my most difficult days, I trust that God is by my side and will give me the wisdom to overcome all obstacles I'm facing."

Ask God every day to help you align your affirmations and actions with His perfect plans for your life.

PROACTIVITY:

Be proactive and choose God's way every day.

You can know God's way through praying, reading the Good Book, and learning from other Christians. Be prepared, set goals, and pursue the plans that God reveals to you through these ways.

Stay positive and make progress on your new journey and mission of continuous improvement and renewal to seek, gain, and apply divine wisdom. To help you, just know that when you wise up, you rise up:

- Every day, seek divine wisdom (not worldly wisdom, but God's wisdom) in your thoughts, decisions, actions, and words. Be wise and understand God's ways.

- Then, apply this divine wisdom to the way you live. Do good works with the humility that comes from wisdom. Have a tremendous work ethic and work WISER to help you soar higher. Gain the wisdom, skill, and will to work for God's good plans for your life.

- When you wise up, you rise up. The Good Book is clear that divine wisdom leads to blessings in your life. Divine wisdom is more valuable than money, gold, silver, and precious jewels, and it can lead to riches, honor, long life (Proverbs 3:13-18, ESV, Proverbs 22:4, Job 28:12-28), good judgment and benefits (Proverbs 9:10-12); and pleasantness and peace (Proverbs 3:17). When you live with divine wisdom, you are bound to be blessed.

Prayer

Pray every day.

Ask God to guide you in all of your thoughts, decisions, actions, and words.

Use this short, simple prayer anytime to start an open and honest chat with God about divine wisdom:

"Father God, it's me, [your name].

Thank You for your gift of wisdom. I want to trust in You with all my heart and not depend on the world or my own understanding. Please be with me as I seek divine wisdom in all I do, and show me which path to take.

In Jesus's name, Amen."

7

NO FEAR: BE STRONG & COURAGEOUS

~~~

Point to Ponder

The command "Do not be afraid" is powerful and appears in the Good Book hundreds of times. Of course, we all experience fear at some point in our lives, and God knows that. After all, He made fear one of the many emotions that humans experience in certain moments. So, what's the best way to overcome fear and be strong and courageous in the moment?

Think about the following **Words of Wisdom**:

"For *God has not given us a spirit of fear* and timidity, but of power, love, and self-discipline." (emphasis added)

Those wise words came from the New Testament: **2 Timothy 1:7**, and they apply to your seventh building block for your House of Faith.

BUILDING BLOCK #7:
NO FEAR: BE STRONG & COURAGEOUS

God does not want us to be afraid of the world and all of its problems. Instead, He wants us to have faith, pray, and be strong and courageous. Simply put, He wants us to overcome fear.

We all experience fear at some point in our lives, and that's okay. Even Jesus experienced fear. On His last day on earth, He knew what He needed to do to save humanity, but His human body was afraid of the painful death He knew He would suffer on the cross. But in the end, He endured and did it anyway... He had faith. He prayed: "...My Father, if it is possible, take this cup of suffering away from me. But let what you want be done, not what I want" (Matthew 26:39, NIRV). He was strong and courageous as He went to the cross. Do you know what we now call that day? We call it "Good Friday," the Friday before Easter.

It's okay to be scared. Life's not about totally avoiding fear. It's about being strong and courageous when you are afraid.

When you're afraid, God wants you to reframe your perspective. To overcome what is facing you, focus on Him and not on fear, worry, or anxiety.

For example, when I flunked out of college at 19 years old, I was a wreck and definitely afraid for my future. I spent months depressed after I was forced to leave college and go back home to my old room in my mom's house with my academic tail between my legs. After a few months of letting me feel sorry for myself, my awesome, faithful, and wise mom shared a powerful Old Testament passage with me: Deuteronomy 28. That passage clearly sets out the different blessings when you obey God and the different curses when you don't.

Man, that was an eye-opener! I quickly reframed my perspective to focus on obeying God and not on my fears or anxiety about my future. I read Deuteronomy 28 and explored the Good Book through different devotional studies nearly every day until I got back on my feet and graduated from both college and law school with high academic honors. That passage and others from the Good Book might be able to help you overcome your fears, too.

BUILDING BY THE GOOD BOOK

What does the Good Book say about having no fear and being strong and courageous instead? It offers encouragement and advice for this new building block in your life by providing strength and support in the Word of God.

These powerful and inspirational verses will help you have no fear and be strong and courageous in all circumstances through Jesus Christ:

- "...**Don't be afraid**. Just have **faith**."

  —Mark 5:36 (emphasis added)

  » **How does this apply to you?** God's power gives you the ability to overcome fear. You just need to have faith in Him. In this verse, Jesus is speaking to a man named Jairus, who had just been told by a crowd of witnesses that his little 12-year-old daughter was dead and that there was no use troubling Jesus. But Jesus overheard them and said to Jairus, "Don't be afraid; just have faith." Afterward, Jesus went to the side of the little girl's bed, held her hand, and miraculously brought her back to life! All of the doubters were overwhelmed and totally amazed. Through faith, which you'll learn more about in the final building block, you have access to God's miraculous power and can overcome any fear.

- "...So *don't be afraid*; you are more valuable to God than a whole flock of sparrows."

  —Luke 12:7 (emphasis added)

  » **How does this apply to you?** God's love gives you the ability to overcome fear. God loves you, cares for you, and wants you to give all of your fears and worries to Him. In this verse, Jesus is clearly saying, "Do not be afraid. You are extremely valuable to me... more than you know." In Jesus's time, sparrows were a valuable trading item. Here, He made the point that God loves and cares about every single sparrow but that you are more valuable to Him than a whole flock of them.

  » In a later book, Jesus's disciple John explained, "We know how much God loves us, and we have put our trust in his love. God is love... And as we live in God, our love grows more perfect... *Such love has no fear*" (1 John 4:16-18, emphasis added). Because He didn't want us enslaved to fear, anxiety, or sin, He sacrificed Himself so that love could win. Through God's perfect love, you have the ability to overcome all fear.

- "I am leaving you with a gift—peace of mind and heart. And the peace I give is a gift the world cannot give. *So, don't be troubled or afraid*."

  —John 14:27 (emphasis added)

» **How does this apply to you?** God's peace gives you the ability to overcome fear. When you're under pressure, always go to God, give Him your fears and struggles, and receive His gift of peace in return. Nothing in this world can replace God's perfect peace.

These are just a few verses in the Good Book that will help you live by faith and trust in God at all times through the ups and downs in life. As you continue to grow in your faith, there are many more that you will learn along the way.

Here are some practical tools for you to continue building your House of Faith and to help you apply the No Fear building block to your life.

BUILDER TOOLKIT APP (AFFIRMATION. PROACTIVITY. PRAYER.)

AFFIRMATION:

Affirm and activate your power to have no fear and be strong and courageous instead. One simple way is to say this easy, powerful phrase to yourself every day:

"God has given me the power, love, and self-discipline to overcome fear. His perfect peace guards my heart and mind. I can do all things through Him who strengthens me."

Ask God every day to help you align your affirmations and actions with His perfect plans for your life.

PROACTIVITY:

Be proactive and choose God's way every day.

You can know God's way through praying, reading the Good Book, and learning from other Christians. Be prepared, set goals, and pursue the plans that God reveals to you through these ways.

Stay positive and make progress on your new journey and mission of continuous improvement and renewal to have no fear and be strong and courageous instead. To help you, just know that you've got the power.

Philippians 4 in the Good Book has the perfect set of useful and practical daily tools to help you. Check out these cool "Philippians Power Tools!"

- "Don't worry about anything; instead, pray about everything. Tell God what you need, and thank him for all he has done. Then you will experience God's peace, which exceeds anything we can understand. His peace will guard your hearts and minds as you live in Christ Jesus."

    —Philippians 4:6-7

- "For I can do everything through Christ, who gives me strength."

    —Philippians 4:13

- "And this same God who takes care of me will supply all your needs from his glorious riches, which have been given to us in Christ Jesus."

    —Philippians 4:19

Simply put, pray about everything. Tell God what you need and thank Him. And know that God will take care of you and supply all your needs.

Every day, use these Philippians Power Tools to keep building the No Fear building block for your House of Faith. You can do *everything, anything, and all things* through Jesus Christ, who strengthens you!

• Prayer •

Pray every day.

Ask God to guide you in all of your thoughts, decisions, actions, and words.

Use this short, simple prayer anytime to start an open and honest chat with God about having no fear and being strong and courageous instead:

ରଃ

"Father God, it's me, [your name].

Thank You for the gift of power, love, and self-discipline to overcome any fear, anxiety, and stress. I put all my faith and trust in You and follow You. Please give me Your perfect peace to always say with confidence, 'God is my Helper and Protector, so I will have no fear. What can people do to me? What is impossible for people is possible with God.'

In Jesus's name, Amen."

THIRD LEVEL:
THE LOFT

The third level of your **F.O.U.N.D.A.T.I.O.N.** has two building blocks. These two blocks form the loft of your House of Faith. **They help you aspire to higher levels of living in Faith.**

Building Blocks for the Third Level: The Loft

- **Uniqueness**
- **Oneness**

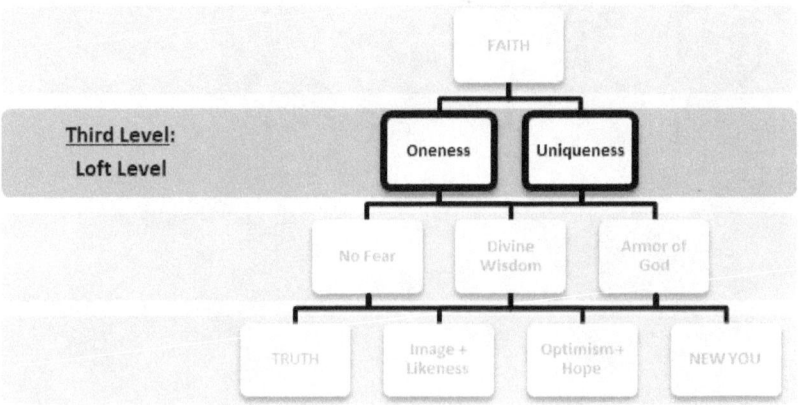

8

UNIQUENESS

Point to Ponder

Earlier in our book, you learned that you are *unique*. God made you for a unique purpose and gave you unique gifts and talents to do good works in this world.

Your uniqueness is the basis of your superpower. It is the beginning of your origin story. Before you were even born, God intentionally and thoughtfully created you to be different and unique from every human on this planet, and He gave you a purpose.

Think about the following **Words of Wisdom**:

"There are *different kinds of spiritual gifts*, but the same Spirit is the source of them all. There are different kinds of service, but we serve the same Lord. God works in different ways, but it is the same God who does the work in all of us. *A spiritual gift is given to each of us so we can help each other*." (emphasis added)

Those wise words came from the New Testament: **1 Corinthians 12:4-7**, and they apply to your eighth building block for your House of Faith.

BUILDING BLOCK #8:
UNIQUENESS

As a teen, one of my favorite 1980s superhero cartoons was "Masters of the Universe."[2] The main hero was Prince Adam, an everyday prince who transformed into He-Man: a big, strong and courageous, bodybuilding-looking, mighty warrior. Prince Adam transformed by raising his power sword to the sky and yelling the phrase, "I HAVE THE POWER!" This idea was so popular globally that, later on, a European rap group named Snap created a popular rap song called "The Power."[3] You can look them both up on YouTube... fun stuff!

Anyway, you are WAY more important to God than any 80s cartoon or 90s rap group. In the last building block on No Fear, you learned that God has given you the power to overcome fear and be strong and courageous. In this current building block on Uniqueness, let's dive deeper into how you have unique God-given power, potential, and purpose.

You might be asking yourself, "How do I know my unique God-given gifts and talents?"

- **Prayers**: Start by asking God directly! Look to Him first and foremost.

- **Passions and pastimes**: Ask yourself, what are you passionate about? How do you enjoy spending time? What are you naturally good at?

---

[2] He-Man and the Masters of the Universe." *He-Man and the Masters of the Universe*, created by Lou Scheimer, Filmation, 1983-1985.
[3] Snap! "The Power." *The Madman's Return*, produced by Michael Münzing and Lars Erichson, Arista, 1992.

- **People**: Ask people around you who know you well, like your parents, family, friends, pastors, and teachers/counselors. Look to others, but remember to listen to their advice through your newfound lens of divine wisdom.

God is clear about the importance of using your unique God-given gifts to better yourself, give back, and benefit others. In doing so, you will be fulfilling your God-given purpose and building the best version of your unique life.

Your uniqueness matters. Your difference matters. YOU matter.

BUILDING BY THE GOOD BOOK

What does the Good Book say about your uniqueness? It offers encouragement and advice for this new building block in your life by providing strength and support in the Word of God.

These powerful and inspirational verses will help you know and apply your unique God-given gifts and talents through Jesus Christ:

- "In his grace, ***God has given us different gifts*** for doing certain things well..."

  —Romans 12:6 (emphasis added)

  » **How does this apply to you?** The Good Book gives a broad range of examples of gifts and talents that were evident at that time in world history (the ability to teach, give wise advice, heal the sick, speak foreign languages, do miracles, lead others, etc.). Just the same, in today's world, God gave you special gifts and talents. Through faith, you can find and hone your talents to do great things with your life. Discover your unique God-given superpowers, and use them to do good in this world.

- "It is the one and only Spirit who distributes all these gifts. *He alone decides which gift each person should have*... Are we all teachers? Do we all have the ability to do miracles? Do we all have the gift of healing? Do we all have the ability to speak in unknown languages? Do we all have the ability to interpret unknown languages? Of course not! *So you should earnestly desire the most helpful gifts*..."

—1 Corinthians 12:11, 29-31 (emphasis added)

  » **How does this apply to you?** We all have different gifts and talents. Just because someone else has the gift of academics, sports, music, languages, or building and you don't, it doesn't mean you're less important. God wants you to desire and focus on YOUR unique gifts and talents that He has given you. The danger in comparing our own gifts and talents to others is that we might get caught up in greed and envy, which leads to doing things to glorify ourselves instead of using our gifts and talent for good works and God's glory.

- "However, *he has given each one of us a special gift* through the generosity of Christ.... This will continue until we all come to such *unity in our faith and knowledge of God's Son* that we will be mature in the Lord, measuring up to the full and complete standard of Christ. Then, we will no longer be immature like children. We won't be tossed and blown about by every wind of new teaching. We will not be influenced when people try to trick us with lies so clever they sound like the truth. Instead, we will *speak the truth in love, growing in every way more and more like Christ, who is the head of His body, the church."*

—Ephesians 4:7, 13-15 (emphasis added)

» **How does this apply to you?** In addition to God-given gifts, some other important concepts here tie into our House of Faith: Unity, Faith, God's Son Jesus, Truth, and Love. As you start to lay your Uniqueness and Oneness building blocks in the Loft level of your House of Faith, everything starts to come together and you can see how these building blocks help you aspire to higher levels of living in Faith.

Another important concept here is how to use our God-given gifts in our relationship with Jesus. C.S. Lewis, the author of the *Chronicles of Narnia* books and a strong Christian, once famously said, "You ask 'for what' God wants you. Of course, He may have a special job for you: and the certain job is that of becoming more and more His."[4] C.S. Lewis makes it very clear: though, yes, God has given us awesome, divine, special assignments and jobs, Jesus sought us out, not because of these special jobs, but because He desires that we become more and more His and more and more like Him. You were graciously given gifts and talents through the generosity of Jesus. Every day, you should give Jesus what He desires - all of you!

These are just a few verses in the Good Book that will help you live by faith and trust in God at all times through the ups and downs in life. As you continue to grow in your faith, there are many more that you will learn along the way.

---

[4] Lewis, C.S. *Mere Christianity*. HarperCollins, 2001.

Here are some practical tools for you to continue building your House of Faith and to help you apply the Uniqueness building block to your life.

BUILDER TOOLKIT APP
(AFFIRMATION. PROACTIVITY. PRAYER.)

AFFIRMATION:

Affirm and activate your uniqueness. One simple way is to say this easy, powerful phrase to yourself every day:

"I am unique. God created me on purpose, for a purpose. I am not a mistake. I am God's thoughtfully and carefully designed creation with unique purpose and gifts. Through Him, I HAVE THE POWER."

Ask God every day to help you align your affirmations and actions with His perfect plans for your life.

PROACTIVITY:

Be proactive and choose God's way every day.

You can know God's way through praying, reading the Good Book, and learning from other Christians. Be prepared, set goals, and pursue the plans that God reveals to you through these ways.

Stay positive and make progress on your new journey and mission of continuous improvement and renewal to find and apply your unique God-given gifts and talents. To help you, just remember that Romans 12:6 says that God has given us all different gifts for doing certain things well.

Use your unique God-given gifts and talents to excel and do well for yourself and others with faith as the foundation for your life.

How? Simple – just serve, shine, and share:

- First, use your unique gifts to *serve* and help others,

- Then, *shine* and reflect God's love to those around you as you do what you're gifted and good at,

- And finally, *share* with others what God has done for you and your personal life.

Prayer

Pray every day.

Ask God to guide you in all of your thoughts, decisions, actions, and words.

Use this short, simple prayer anytime to start an open and honest chat with God about your uniqueness:

ଔ

"Father God, it's me, [your name].

Thank You for thoughtfully and carefully creating me with unique purpose and gifts. I want to use them for Your good and glory. Please help me to always see myself the way that You see me, and show me how I can take part in the special plans and good works You are preparing me uniquely to do.

In Jesus's name, Amen."

9

ONENESS

• Point to Ponder •

In the previous building block, you learned that your individual uniqueness matters to God. He created you for a unique purpose and gave you special gifts to fulfill that purpose.

But did you know that God also intentionally created you to have a strong and meaningful connection with others? Specifically, He wants you to use your individual unique talents in unity with others for the collective good and His glory. I like to call this "**oneness.**"

Think about the following **Words of Wisdom**:

"For there is *one body* and *one Spirit*, just as *you have been called to one glorious hope for the future*. There is *one Lord, one faith, one baptism, one God and Father of all*, who is over all, in all, and living through all." (emphasis added)

Those wise words came from the New Testament: **Ephesians 4:4-6**, and they apply to your ninth building block for your House of Faith.

BUILDING BLOCK #9:
ONENESS

There is so much power in being ONE – working together as one united group to achieve something great and being a unique and special part of something bigger than us all.

To help you think through a modern approach to oneness, did you know that two of the most successful coaches in football history are good friends and shared winning strategies with each other while winning championships with different teams? One coach has the most championships ever in NCAA college football, and the other coach has the most championships ever in NFL pro football. Even though they coached at different levels of the sport, they both taught their championship players and teams one main winning strategy: if each player does their unique individual job to the best of their abilities, then the entire team will win as one. By doing your unique individual job on a team to the best of your abilities, you improve team unity because you allow the next person to do their own job without worrying about needing to pick up the slack.

These two legendary coaches understood that every player was unique, each with a specific role, but they all needed to collaborate as one cohesive team to achieve victory. They often refer to it as "Just do your job."

You know who created that winning strategy before they did? God.

Jesus is the champion who initiates and perfects our faith (Hebrews 12:2). As individual followers of Jesus, each with our own unique, special gifts, we are meant to work together as one body in Christ. This is our championship team. And on our championship team, you matter. God has given you unique individual gifts and talents to do your job so our team can win as ONE.

One of Jesus's greatest followers, the apostle Paul, referred to it as "one body with many parts." Paul used the human body as an analogy to show how Christians, each with their own unique special gifts, are meant to work together in unity as one. He said it multiple times in different ways to encourage the early Christians who were spread out in different cities in the Roman Empire:

- "Just as our bodies have many parts and each part has a special function, so it is with Christ's body. We are many parts of *one body*, and *we all belong to each other*."

  —Romans 12:4-5 (emphasis added)

- "The human body has many parts, but the many parts make up *one whole body*. So it is with the body of Christ."

  —1 Corinthians 12:12 (emphasis added)

BUILDING BY THE GOOD BOOK

What else does the Good Book say about oneness? It offers encouragement and advice for this new building block in your life by providing strength and support in the Word of God.

These powerful and inspirational verses will help you know and understand that you are a unique and valuable part of one body with God and the church through Jesus Christ:

- "God has put all things under the authority of Christ and has *made him head over all things* for the benefit of the church. And *the church is His body*; it is made full and complete by Christ, who fills all things everywhere with himself."

—Ephesians 1:22-23 (emphasis added)

» **How does this apply to you?** God put all things under the authority of Jesus and made Him head over all things for the benefit of the church. The church is His body, and it is made full and complete by Jesus. With Jesus as the head of your life, you have the perfect leader and example to follow and serve. As you fulfill your unique purpose and do your unique part, you will improve your life and the lives of those around you, including your family, friends, classmates, church, and, ultimately, the world.

• "But our bodies have many parts, and God has put each part just where he wants it. How strange a body would be if it had only one part! Yes, there are many parts, but *only one body*... In fact, some parts of the body that seem weakest and least important are actually the most necessary... So God has put the body together such that extra honor and care are given to those parts that have less dignity. This makes for harmony among the members, so that all of the members care for each other. If one part suffers, all the parts suffer with it, and if one part is honored, all the parts are glad. *All of you together are Christ's body, and each of you is a part of it*."

—1 Corinthians 12:18-20, 22, 24-27 (emphasis added)

» **How does this apply to you?** You are not isolated, alone, or disconnected. You are a part of one body with many members. You are part of a team: a championship team.

All of us together are Christ's body, and each one of us is a unique part of it. God put each of us exactly where He wants us, and just like on a team, if one of us does well, then all of us do well, and if one of us suffers, then all of us suffer. You are extremely important and valuable to the team, no matter what your job is (even if you're the equipment manager on a football team). God is clear that some parts of the body that seem weakest and least important are actually the most necessary. For example, "And if the ear says, 'I am not part of the body because I am not an eye,' would that make it any less a part of the body? If the whole body was an eye, how would you hear? Or if your whole body were an ear, how would you smell anything?" (1 Corinthians 12:16-17). You matter to God's team.

- "Their responsibility is to equip God's people to do his work and build up the church, **the body of Christ**... He makes **the whole body** fit together perfectly. As each part does its own special work, it helps the other parts grow, so that **the whole body** is healthy and growing and full of love."

—Ephesians 4:12, 16 (emphasis added)

» **How does this apply to you?** God made the whole body fit together perfectly. Since Jesus is the head of the body, we are called to grow in every way more and more like Jesus. God composed the body so that its parts care for each other. As each part does its own special work, it helps the other parts grow so that the whole body is healthy and full of harmony.

These are just a few verses in the Good Book that will help you live by faith and trust in God at all times through the ups and downs in life. As you continue to grow in your faith, there are many more that you will learn along the way.

Here are some practical tools for you to continue building your House of Faith and to help you apply the Oneness building block to your life.

BUILDER TOOLKIT APP (AFFIRMATION. PROACTIVITY. PRAYER.)

AFFIRMATION:

Affirm and activate your oneness with God and others. One simple way is to say this easy, powerful phrase to yourself every day:

"I am one with God; God is one with me. Jesus Christ is the head of His body, and I fit together perfectly with the other parts of His body. I am not isolated, alone, or disconnected. As I do my own unique job, I help the other parts grow so that the whole body is healthy."

Ask God every day to help you align your affirmations and actions with His perfect plans for your life.

PROACTIVITY:

Be proactive and choose God's way every day.

You can know God's way through praying, reading the Good Book, and learning from other Christians. Be prepared, set goals, and pursue the plans that God reveals to you through these ways.

Stay positive and make progress on your new journey and mission of continuous improvement and renewal to help your oneness with God and others. To help you, just remember the power of ONE. Paul said it in this practical way:

> "And let the peace that comes from Christ rule in your hearts. For as **members of one body** you are called to live in peace. And always be thankful. Let the message about Christ, in all its richness, fill your lives. Teach and counsel each other with all the wisdom He gives. Sing psalms and hymns and spiritual songs to God with thankful hearts. And whatever you do or say, do it as a representative of the Lord Jesus, giving thanks through Him to God the Father."
>
> —Colossians 3:15-17 (emphasis added)

In other words, let God's perfect peace rule within you, always thank Him, and let the Good News of Jesus Christ fill your life. And whatever you do or say, as a member of our team, do your job as a representative of our Lord Jesus so our team can win as ONE: "... one Lord, one faith, one baptism, one God and Father of all, who is over all, in all, and living through all" (Ephesians 4:5-6).

Your uniqueness matters to our oneness.

Prayer

Pray every day.

Ask God to guide you in all of your thoughts, decisions, actions, and words.

Use this short, simple prayer anytime to start an open and honest chat with God about oneness with God and others:

"Father God, it's me, [your name].

Thank You for making me a part of your championship team. I want to use my unique God-given gifts and talents to excel and do well for myself, others, and the body of Christ. Please show me how our oneness creates opportunities for me to do good works for your glory every day. I want us to WIN as ONE.

In Jesus's name. Amen."

FINAL LEVEL:

THE ROOFTOP

The fourth and final level of your **F.O.U.N.D.A.T.I.O.N.** has one building block. This single block forms the rooftop of your House of Faith.

It is the highpoint in how to live your best life. It is your covering and protection from above.

Building Block for the Final Level: The Rooftop

- **FAITH**

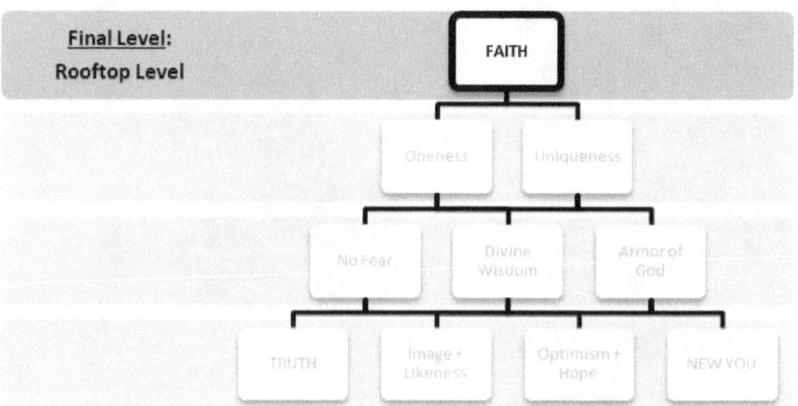

10

FOUNDATION BUILDING BLOCK

FAITH

• Point to Ponder •

Have you heard The Good News?

The Good News will help you live your best life ever... Guaranteed.

The Good News is the power of God at work, saving everyone who believes.

The Good News tells us how God makes us right in His sight.

The Good News is about **Jesus Christ**, and it is through **faith** in Him that a person has **life**.

Think about the following final **Words of Wisdom**:

"For I am not ashamed of *this Good News about Christ*. It is the power of God at work, saving everyone who believes... This Good News tells us how God makes us right in his sight. ***This is accomplished from start to finish by faith***. As the Scriptures say, 'It is through *faith* that a righteous person has *life*.'" (emphasis added)

Those wise words came from the New Testament: **Romans 1:16-17**, and they apply to your tenth and final building block for your House of Faith.

BUILDING BLOCK #10:
FAITH

Earlier in this book, I promised to give you building blocks for the foundation of a supremely strong structure. A house that is so strong that when the heavy storms of life come, it stands tall and does not fall: a House of Faith.

Faith is powerful. It is an overarching, primary principle that Jesus Himself said that you must have in everyday life. And, He didn't say it once... He said and demonstrated it numerous times and in numerous ways to many different people he encountered, including everyone from His close disciples to complete strangers.

Here are five short stories where Jesus taught people about the power of faith:

1. **To His disciples:** "And Jesus answered them, "Truly, I say to you, *if you have faith* and do not doubt, you will not only do what has been done to the fig tree, but even if you say to this mountain, 'Be taken up and thrown into the sea,' it will happen. And whatever you ask in prayer, you will receive, *if you have faith.*'"
—Matthew 21:21-22, ESV (emphasis added)

2. **To a blind man**: "And Jesus stopped and said, "Call him." And they called the blind man, saying to him, "Take heart. Get up; he is calling you." And throwing off his cloak, he sprang up and came to Jesus. And Jesus said to him, "What do you want me to do for you?" And the blind man said to him, "Rabbi, let me recover my sight." And Jesus said to him, "Go your way; *your faith has made you well.*"

And immediately he recovered his sight and followed him on the way."
—Mark 10:49-52, ESV (emphasis added)

3. **In the middle of a raging storm at sea:** "The disciples went and woke him up, shouting, 'Master, Master, we're going to drown!' When Jesus woke up, he rebuked the wind and the raging waves. Suddenly the storm stopped and all was calm. Then he asked them, *'Where is your faith?'* The disciples were terrified and amazed. 'Who is this man?' they asked each other. 'When he gives a command, even the wind and waves obey him!'"
—Luke 8:24-25 (emphasis added)

4. **To a diseased woman:** "When the woman realized that she could not stay hidden, she began to tremble and fell to her knees in front of him. The whole crowd heard her explain why she had touched him and that she had been immediately healed. 'Daughter,' he said to her, *'your faith has made you well.* Go in peace.'"
—Luke 8:47-48 (emphasis added)

5. **In response to a direct question about faith:** "The apostles said to the Lord, *'Show us how to increase our faith.'* The Lord answered, *'If you had faith even as small as a mustard seed*, you could say to this mulberry tree, 'May you be uprooted and be planted in the sea,' and it would obey you!"
—Luke 17:5-6 (emphasis added)

You get the point. The list goes on and on. When you have faith, you have power in the mighty name of Jesus.

Finally, faith is an essential life force, not a lofty goal to achieve and then move on from. It is a lifelong and eternal covering and protection from above, and it forms the rooftop of your House of Faith. It is also one of the three key building blocks that keep all of the other building blocks in alignment. The other two are the Truth building block and the New You building block. As you'll see in the conclusion of this book, these three building blocks — **Faith**, **Truth**, and **New You** — work together in a 360-degree synergistic cycle that transforms your life in positive and eternal ways.

BUILDING BY THE GOOD BOOK

What does the Good Book say about Faith? It offers encouragement and advice for this final building block in your life by providing strength and support in the Word of God.

These powerful and inspirational verses will help you have FAITH in God in all circumstances through Jesus Christ:

- "So *faith* comes from hearing, that is, hearing the Good News about Christ."

  —Romans 10:17 (emphasis added)

  » **How does this apply to you? Faith is easy for you to obtain.** Faith comes from hearing the Good News about Christ. It's already been shared with you here. You've just got to hear and believe the truth about Jesus. If you don't find belief that easy, then listen in other ways. Sometimes, God speaks through your thoughts, prayers, or dreams. Sometimes, He speaks through other people or circumstances. Don't be discouraged. Listen to Jesus's teaching and follow it. It might take time, but it will click, and you will find your faith in Him.

And when you're ready (trust me, you'll know), then you've got to share the Good News with others. Sharing the Good News is called the Great Commission: "...Go into all the world and preach the Good News to everyone" (Mark 16:15). Paul said it this way in his letter to the Romans: "For 'Everyone who calls on the name of the Lord will be saved.' But how can they call on Him to save them unless they **believe in Him**? And how can they believe in Him if they have never **heard about Him**? And how can they hear about Him **unless someone tells them**? And how will anyone go and tell them without being sent? That is why the Scriptures say, 'How beautiful are the feet of messengers who bring good news!'" (Romans 10:13-15, emphasis added). Share the Good News with genuine joy.

- "Therefore, since we have been justified **by faith**, we have peace with God through our Lord Jesus Christ. Through him we have also obtained access **by faith** into this grace in which we stand, and we rejoice in hope of the glory of God."
—Romans 5:1-2, ESV (emphasis added)

  » **How does this apply to you? Faith gives you access to God.** By faith, you have peace with God through Jesus Christ. Through Jesus, you obtain access by faith into God's grace, and you can rejoice in the hope of the glory of God. In the Book of Hebrews, Paul said it this way: "And it is impossible to please God without **faith**. Anyone who wants to come to him must **believe that God exists** and that **he rewards those who sincerely seek him**" (Hebrews 11:6, emphasis added). God rewards those who sincerely have faith in Him.

- "So be truly glad. There is wonderful joy ahead, even though you must endure many trials for a little while. These trials will show that *your faith* is genuine. It is being tested as fire tests and purifies gold—though *your faith* is far more precious than mere gold. So when *your faith* remains strong through many trials, it will bring you much praise and glory and honor on the day when Jesus Christ is revealed to the whole world."
  —1 Peter 1:6-7 (emphasis added)

  » **How does this apply to you? Faith is a powerful and valuable force that gets stronger and mightier through hard times.** It is more precious than gold, and it will bring you praise, glory, and honor when you endure trials and are strong. Faith is so powerful that you can even be full of great joy when you go through hard times! Paul said it this way: "Dear brothers and sisters, when troubles of any kind come your way, consider it an opportunity for great joy. For you know that when *your faith* is tested, your endurance has a chance to grow. So let it grow, for when your endurance is fully developed, you will be perfect and complete, needing nothing" (James 1:2-4, emphasis added). When your faith is tested, you will grow stronger.

- "But *the Lord is faithful*; he will strengthen you and guard you from the evil one."
  —2 Thessalonians 3:3 (emphasis added)

  » **How does this apply to you? Faith goes both ways.** God is *always* faithful to us. In return, we just need to have faith in Him and be faithful to Him. Similar to the verses above about your faith being tested, when you're under attack from the enemy, remember that God is faithful and will strengthen and protect you. Just put on the full Armor of God, remember the Truth, and stand your ground against the enemy and his lies!

- "But that does not mean we want to dominate you by telling you *how to put your faith into practice*. We want to work together with you so you will be full of joy, for *it is by your own faith that you stand firm*."
  —2 Corinthians 1:24 (emphasis added)

  » **How does this apply to you? Faith makes you stand firm.** It's up to you how to put your faith into practice. Faith is ultimately a personal decision because you alone must decide to believe, accept, and follow Jesus. But when you decide to do so, you will become the best man you could possibly ever be. And when you have faith and follow God's ways, you will stand firm in life. When the storms come, you will be a house that stands tall and does not fall!

These are just a few verses in the Good Book that will help you live by faith and trust in God at all times through the ups and downs in life. As you continue to grow in your faith, there are many more that you will learn along the way.

Here are some practical tools for you to continue building your House of Faith and to help you apply the Faith building block to your life.

BUILDER TOOLKIT APP
(AFFIRMATION. PROACTIVITY. PRAYER.)
AFFIRMATION:

Affirm and activate your Faith. One simple way is to say this easy, powerful phrase to yourself every day:

> **"I have faith in GOD, through my Lord and Savior, Jesus Christ. I live my life by faith, not by sight."**

Ask God every day to help you align your affirmations and actions with His perfect plans for your life.

PROACTIVITY:

Be proactive and choose God's way every day.

You can know God's way through praying, reading the Good Book, and learning from other Christians. Be prepared, set goals, and pursue the plans that God reveals to you through these ways.

Stay positive and make progress on your new journey and mission of continuous improvement and renewal to your life of Faith. Just build your house on solid rock.

This is the essence of the House of Faith. Jesus said, "Anyone who listens to my teaching and follows it is wise, like a person who **builds a house on solid rock.**"

(Matthew 7:24, emphasis added)

Each of the ten life lessons you've learned in this book is a building block for the foundation of your House of Faith. The ten building blocks spell out the word F.O.U.N.D.A.T.I.O.N.:

FAITH
Oneness
Uniqueness
No Fear: Be Strong & Courageous
Divine Wisdom
Armor of God
TRUTH (The Cornerstone)
Image + Likeness
Optimism + Hope
NEW YOU

Every day, revisit and use all ten of these life lessons and building blocks to build a foundation that will help you improve your life and build your unique House of Faith.

• Prayer •

Pray every day.

Ask God to guide you in all of your thoughts, decisions, actions, and words.

Use this short, simple prayer anytime to start an open and honest chat with God about your Faith:

ೱ

"Father God, it's me, [your name].

Thank You for your faithfulness. I have total faith in You, and it's way more than the size of a mustard seed! I love you God, and I want to always be faithful and right in your sight. Thank you for making life so simple: Love God, love people, share the Good News. Please bless me to always have faith in You.

In Jesus's name, Amen."

THE FOUND BOYS - BUILDING PROJECT COMPLETION:

FOUNDED BY FAITH. WELDED BY WISDOM. BUILT BY GOD.

"In his kindness God called you to share in his eternal glory by means of Christ Jesus... he will restore, support, and strengthen you, and he will place you on a ***firm foundation***. All power to him forever! Amen."

—1 Peter 5:10-11 (emphasis added)

Congratulations, you did it! Well done, good and faithful young man!

You followed the blueprint and completed your learning project about the ten building blocks to the House of Faith. This is just the beginning as you learn to apply these valuable life lessons to your life daily and consistently.

Your House of Faith is a strong castle in the Kingdom of God... founded by faith, welded by wisdom, and built by God. As you follow Jesus and build your House of Faith, you are being built into God's spiritual temple (1 Peter 2:5).

THE THREE KEY BUILDING BLOCKS

Now that you're on your journey to build your House of Faith, you should know the three key building blocks to your Kingdom castle.

When you look at our blueprint image of the House of Faith, you might notice that I put the three corners of the House of Faith in all caps:

FAITH <—> TRUTH <—> NEW YOU

That's because these three blocks are key to building your Kingdom castle, and they are connected in a 360-degree synergistic cycle.

The Good Book summarizes this in a cool way:

"For everyone who has been ***born of God*** overcomes the world. And this is the victory that has overcome the world – ***our faith***. Who is it that overcomes the world except the one who ***believes that Jesus is the Son of God***?"
—1 John 5:4-5, ESV (emphasis added)

In other words, everyone who is born of God (that is, the **New You**) overcomes the world through their **Faith** and belief in the **Truth**: Jesus, the Son of God. Faith is confidence in what we hope for and assurance about what we do not see (Hebrews 11:1). Jesus is the Truth and Cornerstone: the first and primary block for you to focus on and apply in your House of Faith. The New You is the new person you become through Faith and Truth, and who actively works on all ten of the building blocks to keep your House of Faith in order and alignment.

It's all a reciprocal cycle. Your F.O.U.N.D.A.T.I.O.N. has been laid, and your learning project is complete. You are ready for life's storms and the sunshine, bad times and good times.

In our Father's House, there's always a place for you. And remember, a house is often a beacon of light to weary travelers on dark roads in the wilderness.

With your new House of Faith, *be a light in this world*.

WE ARE THE FOUND BOYS

You are on your way to becoming a faithful, wise, and mighty young man. Founded by Faith. Welded by Wisdom. Built by God.

The mission is simple. Follow Jesus. Love God. Love people. Share the Good News. You have the tools. Pray to God, read the Good Book, and continue to build your House.

You just gotta have faith, and enjoy the journey.

And above all: every day, live, love, and lead like Jesus.

***

- We must forge and guard this house. -

THE HOUSE OF FAITH
ESTABLISH YOUR FOUNDATION

FAITH

Oneness | **U**niqueness

No Fear | **D**ivine Wisdom | **A**rmor of God

TRUTH (The Cornerstone) | **I**mage + Likeness | **O**ptimism + Hope | **N**EW YOU

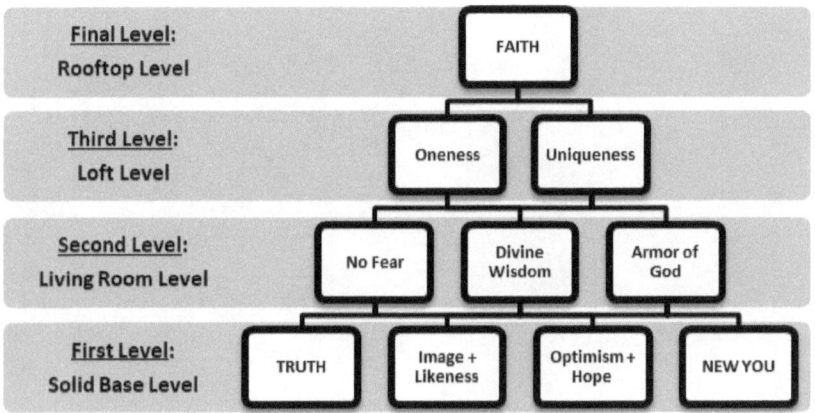

Follow The Found Boys podcast

on Spotify, Apple, or wherever you listen to podcasts to make it part of your life and let it inspire and ignite you.